THE CIRCLE OF SIMPLICITY

"For those who want to simplify their lives—solo or in the context of a simplicity circle—*The Circle of Simplicity* is a terrific starting point. It is at once a simplicity primer and compendium of advice, insight, and critique of our culture of consumerism. The book provides both guidance and inspiration for those who want to get off the fast track and learn how to become fully alive."

—Wanda Urbanska and Frank Levering,
coauthors of *Moving to a Small Town* and *Simple Living*

"*The Circle of Simplicity* is a valuable guidebook to living better now—not through having more of what Madison Avenue thinks you should have, but by finding a way of living that is in keeping with your own values, inspirations, and joys. Cecile Andrews' years of work with people struggling to find simpler and more meaningful ways of life provide an immediate sense of the difficulties and rewards to be found in moving towards a life of voluntary simplicity."

—Sarah van Gelder, editor,
Yes! A Journal of Positive Futures

THE CIRCLE OF SIMPLICITY

RETURN TO THE GOOD LIFE

CECILE ANDREWS

HarperPerennial

A Division of HarperCollins*Publishers*

First HarperPerennial edition published 1998.

Designed by Joseph Rutt

The Library of Congress has catalogued the hardcover edition as follows:

Andrews, Cecile.
    The circle of simplicity : return to the good life / by Cecile
Andrews. — 1st ed.
        p.   cm.
    Includes bibliographical references.
    ISBN 0-06-017814-0
    1. Simplicity.   2. Spiritual life.   I. Title.
BJ1496.A53   1997
646.7—dc21   96-51531

ISBN 0-06-092872-7 (pbk.)

01 02 ❖/RRD 10 9

This book is dedicated to my wonderful family—my husband, Paul; my children, Daniel and Rebecca; my sister, Mary, and her son, Jonathon; and to the memory of my mother, Margaret Tisdel MacFarlane, 1913–1990

She would have been so pleased

At least 10 percent of my proceeds from this book will be used to help establish the Northwest School of Sustainability—a school dedicated to spreading the ideas in this book

CONTENTS

PREFACE

In 1989, I offered a workshop at a community college in Seattle on the subject of voluntary simplicity. Only four people registered.

Three years later, in 1992, I offered the workshop again. This time, 175 people came.

Since then, countless numbers of people throughout the country have been involved in simplicity circles—small groups of people meeting together in homes and schools, working to create lives of well-being for people and the planet. They are building lives of high satisfaction and low environmental impact and rediscovering a way of living that brings joy and fulfillment. They are returning to the good life.

INTRODUCTION

The mass of men lead lives of quiet desperation.
—HENRY DAVID THOREAU

Joan's job was beginning to take up her whole life. She thought about it all the time—usually with a tense, sick feeling in her stomach. And it was not that she was the CEO or anything—just a vice president for an HMO. She just didn't have a feel for what might happen next: would her budget get cut, would her boss bring her another emergency project to be done yesterday, would she even keep her job?

All the cutbacks. She thought her job was secure, but so had Susan. What was Susan going to do now? She and Dave had spent everything they earned, using their five-year-old daughter's college fund for the down payment on the new house.

She hadn't really talked to Susan lately, except to leave voice mail messages about having lunch. Actually, she hadn't seen many of her friends this year. She just couldn't face the effort of having people to dinner—cleaning her house, going through the piles of clutter, or cooking! And it probably wouldn't be any fun anyway; lately there was so much back-biting among her friends at work.

Besides, when could they do it? On Saturdays she and Joel tried to get out of town—even if they took briefcases full of work with them. Theoretically, they left town to spend some time together, but they both kept calling their voice mail, returning calls to everybody else who was catching up on office work. They might as well stay home—the calls would be cheaper.

She had never really worried about money, but lately she had been running up bills—buying things she didn't need, like those new shoes and the bread maker. Bread maker! That was a joke. Another kitchen appliance that would never get used.

She'd been tired a lot, too, and Joel seemed to be particularly irritating lately. Whenever they were together he was always sneaking a look at his watch. She wondered if other couples had such paltry sex lives—falling into bed exhausted at midnight didn't help. They hadn't laughed in a long time, either.

It was the rushing around that drove her crazy. She couldn't seem to stop, even on the weekends. She wished she could just sit and stare into space.

But the worst thing was the Sunday night dread. She would think about Monday morning and work, and her stomach would tighten and jaw muscles clench. Actually, it would start on Saturday, when she wondered whether she could get all her errands done. She'd think: Am I enjoying my time enough? Do I dare go for a walk, or should I do the laundry? The only time she felt free was on Friday night, and she was too tired to enjoy it. They'd be asleep on the couch by 8:30, the television blaring.

Was this it? Wasn't there something more?

A lot of people feel like Joan—rushed and frenzied and stressed. They have no time for their friends; they snap at their family; they're not laughing very much. But a growing number of people aren't content to live this way. They are looking for ways to simplify their lives—to rush less, work less, and spend less. They are beginning to slow down and enjoy life again.

There's a movement associated with this—it's called the voluntary simplicity movement. Around the country, thousands of people are simplifying their lives. They are questioning the standard definitions that equate success with money and prestige and the accumulation of things. They are returning to the good life.

People are attracted to this movement for a lot of different reasons. Many are looking for more time. Some are looking for ways to save money, to find techniques for living on less. Most are searching for more meaning. Almost all are concerned about the environment, for they realize that our lifestyle is leading to the destruction of nature. They're all searching for ways that help them feel excited about life when they awake each morning, ways that help them find joy in the moment, a sense of purpose in their work, ways that help them feel a sense of connection with all of life.

People are moving more slowly, savoring their time, lingering over their meals, conversing with their friends. Listen to their voices:

> For me, voluntary simplicity is living consciously, trying to eliminate the unnecessary, the superficial clutter. It is trying to live morally and ethically in the global economy by using less.

> I think of voluntary simplicity as living on purpose, making sure I have the time to do the things I want to do, not wishing my time away.

> I think that voluntary simplicity is being true to yourself, true to the environment. It's finding that place for every facet of my life and defining how much is enough. For me it is spiritual.

> It's choosing to enhance one's life by surrounding yourself with what really brings you fulfillment. It's defining my own standard of success and prosperity, community and fun.

> Voluntary simplicity is balancing the realities of my life (limited economics, time, and energy) with my values and implementing them into a lifestyle that is comfortable and rewarding. I think voluntary simplicity is an "art of living." I believe it is an art to live, to be true to who you are and to be open to innovation.

These are the words of people in simplicity circles, people of all ages and backgrounds who sense there is a better way than trying to change on their own.

A lot of people are realizing that just reading a book or going to a workshop isn't enough. They get fired up for a few weeks and then they slip back into their old habits. To make lasting, profound changes, people are joining simplicity circles. Simplicity circles are small groups of people who gather together, without experts or authorities, to help each other simplify their lives—to support each other, to think together, to exchange ideas on ways to live differently. When you're working with like-minded people, talking with kindred spirits, exploring with people who share your values, it's easier to make changes.

A NEW APPROACH TO LEARNING

I became involved in the voluntary simplicity movement in the same way many have. I was working all the time but I was beginning to enjoy it less. My work was beginning to grow stale. As a community college administrator, the director of continuing education, I had always thought that I could do important things by developing stimulating, thought-provoking classes for people. But it was getting harder and harder, and I was feeling discouraged and bored.

One year, I had an experience that set my life on a new course. It began with Fall Convocation—the start of another community college school year.

Every year at the beginning of October, I tried to figure out how to get out of this annual fall gathering. The whole school trooped in to hear the president welcome us back, and the address was always uninspiring and full of platitudes, with the president telling us how we were one big family, how students were the most important thing, blah, blah, blah.

Since I was an administrator, I had to go, so I always sat in the front to make sure that the president saw me. To avoid being bored to death, I sat next to a good friend so we could talk surreptitiously, make comments about the inane remarks we were hearing.

This year was different. We had a Native American speaker who told stories about his childhood education, an education that was very different from our mainstream American schools. He said that his grandfather would take him into the woods and have him sit quietly all day watching the beavers. At the end of the day his grandfather would ask him, "What did you see? What did you feel? What did you learn?"

He went on to tell stories about how his education, Native people's education, came from real experiences, not just from books; how what he learned linked him to nature and to his community; how his education transformed him by developing an inner authority. The stories about his people moved everyone to tears. There I was, tears on my cheeks, my nose running, sitting in the front row and no handkerchief. I had expected it to be boring! The room was deeply silent, the way it is when people are totally absorbed, so I couldn't even sniff. I resorted to wiping my nose on my shirtsleeve.

A NEW VISION OF LEARNING AND HUMAN GROWTH

That was the beginning for me of a new approach to learning and renewal. I was crying because his message was moving and inspiring, but there was also a sadness. Why hadn't I had an education like that—an experience of learning that absorbed me and transformed me, that brought me face to face with life? Further, why didn't my work as an educator have that kind of vitality?

The talk on that day gave me a new vision of learning. That vision was the seed that grew into simplicity circles—a new, more exciting, more meaningful way of learning.

ORDINARY PEOPLE CREATE CHANGE

In the last few years, there have been countless stories in the press about the growing voluntary simplicity movement. Because media love the outrageous example, many have come to associate this movement with people who make *drastic* changes—quitting their high paying jobs and living on only a few hundred dollars a month. While these stories can be inspiring, some might conclude that voluntary simplicity is a movement only for the few. Hearing those stories, ordinary people can give up, thinking that they could never do what these people have done, that the voluntary simplicity movement holds nothing for them. But people in simplicity circles discover that everyone can simplify their lives in some way, and that even the small things people do are important and fulfilling. They learn that there is no *one* way to simplify; rather, each person's unique way grows out of an analysis of his or her own life.

Many of the stories in the press perpetuate our fascination with rugged individualism—going against the tide, riding into the sunset. But simplicity circles offer another dimension—a community of searchers. Voluntary simplicity isn't a formula, a list of things to do—it's a search, a search for a new way to live.

Simplicity circles lead to both personal fulfillment and social change. Change doesn't usually start from the top and it isn't initiated by just one person. It is people, in their ordinary lives, who search for answers and make a difference.

A CONVERSATION

In the spirit of simplicity circles, I wrote this book as a conversation, with the understanding that I don't have all the answers myself. I'm looking, just as many are, for a new way to live.

The longer I have been an educator, the more strongly I feel that we must resist giving power over our lives to experts. Experts and authorities silence us, make us quit thinking for ourselves. And when we are silenced, we become passive and lose hope. Only when we all participate will we be able to solve the problems that face us. Only as we all join in conversation, will we begin to participate.

So instead of writing as an expert, I write as a fellow seeker, using my own stories while inviting others to examine their stories, because our truths must be rooted in our own experience. As the German poet Goethe said, "All truly wise thoughts have been thought already thousands of times; but to make them truly ours, we must think them over again honestly, till they take root in our personal experience."

METAPHORS FOR CHANGE

In deciding how to organize this book, I thought about the metaphors that I kept hearing. Some talk about creating a new map. Maps give you directions, tell you which way to go. Our belief systems are like maps—they are the belief systems that we learn that describe reality to us; they tell us how to live, the directions to take. People have discovered that the conventional routes have led us to a barren landscape—they have failed to lead us to the joy and happiness that we thought was our destination. But I realized that it's not a new map I'm looking for. Maybe it's no longer helpful to see life as a journey to a destination.

Others talk about waking up from a bad dream, about learning to see more clearly, removing blinders from their eyes. That metaphor appealed to me, for voluntary simplicity is certainly about reshaping the American Dream.

But the metaphor that kept recurring to me is one of fire—the sense of rekindling our sense of joy in life. I've always loved the poet William Butler Yeats's phrase, "Education is not the filling of a bucket but the starting of a fire." I've always wanted education to rekindle people's spirit, to get them fired up about life.

So, how could I bring these metaphors together without their seeming just a jumble? Something from my childhood kept coming into my mind: when I was young, I was in Campfire Girls, and I've always remembered the ranks they used then—Trail Seeker, Wood Gatherer, Fire Maker, Torch Bearer. I loved those phrases! They still excite me. But how could I use them? I kept thinking it was stupid to use something like that to organize a book, but my husband, a writer, said, No, you have to pay attention when thoughts persist.

And as I thought of these phrases, I saw that I had moved away from the symbol of life as journey to a symbol of life as gathering together in a circle around the fire. When you go camping, you find your place and settle in. You take some trails out to explore, but you always come back. You go out and gather wood along the way, and come back and start the fire. Then, you gather in a circle around the fire to tell stories, to sing, to feel close together, to feel part of the night, part of the nature surrounding you. Ah, I thought. What a perfect metaphor. Telling stories around the fire. Simplicity circles!

So, instead of developing a new map, we will do something more modest—we will seek out our own trails. We'll explore paths that ultimately lead us back to where we began, and there we will build a fire for warmth and light.

But before we set out on the trails, we have to wake up, to understand that we have been half-asleep, taking a direction that we have not chosen. We have to begin to see more clearly, to see what is really important in life.

After waking up, we get ready to set out to seek new trails. We need to clear out the brambles so that we can find the trail head. The second area we explore is clarity—clearing away the clutter from our lives, both the physical and emotional clutter, and cutting back on the demands on our time and reducing consumption.

Then we become trail seekers, searching for a new path to a new way to live, a new philosophy of life. It is our own unique path that we seek—one that leads back to our true selves. We learn to be authentic, to find our passion, and to search our lives for meaning.

As we move along the path, we become wood gatherers. Bringing things together, we create community with other people and with nature.

Next we become fire makers, rekindling our spirit and getting in touch with a deeper spirit of life.

Then we set out as torch bearers to change the larger society, seeking social justice, transforming institutions—carrying the torch to others.

Finally, we gather together in the circle to keep the flames burning, to make changes for the long haul with a group of people who bring us community and a chance to speak about things that matter.

A COUNTRY'S HERITAGE

Gathering around the fire has a special meaning for Americans, because that's the way we began—gathered around the hearth in a house we had built with our own hands or gathered around an open fire under the sky as we set out across the land. When we create a new vision of life, we need to build on what we cherish in our past. To feel a sense of dignity, a nation needs to have a sense of pride in its heritage—we have seen it as African Americans recapture their roots, as women reclaim their history. Our founding fathers and mothers advocated the simple life, warned against excess and shallow materialism, exhorted us to develop the inner life. Along the way, we've forgotten this, but now people are remembering. Recapturing the simple life is a return to the good life.

THE CIRCLE OF SIMPLICITY

PART 1

THE AWAKENING OF SOUL

We can now recognize that the fate of the soul is the fate of the social order; that if the spirit within us withers, so too will all the world we build about us.

—THEODORE ROSZAK

In these last years of the twentieth century, we have reawakened to the concept of soul—it seems as if every other book published has the word *soul* in the title. The theme of these books is that we have lost touch with a depth and substance in life, that we are searching for ways to reclaim an experience of aliveness and authenticity and find a way to return to the good life.

People feel an emptiness, a sense that life isn't all it could be. Albert Schweitzer called it our "sleeping sickness of the soul."

Why a sleeping sickness of the soul? Is it because we have sold our soul for comforts and conveniences, for status and success? It can be painful to examine our lives, but, there are people out there creating a new vision, creating a way of life that involves an awakening of the soul.

THE AMERICAN DREAM

A SLEEPING SICKNESS OF THE SOUL

You know of the disease in Central Africa called
sleeping sickness . . . There also exists a sleeping
sickness of the soul. Its most dangerous aspect is that
one is unaware of its coming. That is why you have to
be careful. As soon as you notice the slightest sign of
indifference, the moment you become aware of the loss
of a certain seriousness, of longing, of enthusiasm and
zest, take it as a warning. You should realize that your
soul suffers if you live superficially.

—ALBERT SCHWEITZER

"Repression of the life force" is a diagnosis I believe
would fit most of the emotional problems people
present in therapy."

—THOMAS MOORE

Let's look at some facts about life in America today.

First, there's no time:

- Couples spend an average of twelve minutes a day talking to
  each other.

- We spend forty minutes a week playing with children.

- Half of Americans don't get enough sleep.

We feel like we are constantly rushing. And for good reason: as
a society we are working longer hours than we ever have before.
Harvard researcher Juliet Schor has estimated that we are working

one month more per year than we did twenty years ago.

Even one month doesn't seem like it could be right. Those averages tell us little about individual lives. Some people are working fifty or sixty or seventy hours per week. And it depends how you measure it. Is it just the hours at the office or all the things you do at home—the calls you make, the paperwork, the hours spent worrying in the middle of the night? Whatever the real hours are, for most of us, it's too much.

It's not just the lack of time. We've lost our *joie de vivre*. Our *life force is repressed*. There's so little that we feel passionate about, so little that brings us joy. We don't laugh much or sing or dance much.

THE BIZZARENESS OF MODERN LIFE

Although our lives seem normal to us, when you look closely they appear bizarre. Yet we accept the unacceptable. We show no surprise about these daily features of our lives:

- Instead of spending long hours over dinner with friends, we eat with one hand while we're driving.

- When making a call, most of us would rather get an answering machine than talk to a real person.

- People are falling in love and courting through the computer.

- Small towns vie to have prisons built in their area in order to secure jobs.

People are always shocked when I tell them about something I read about Japan—about young couples hiring a family to visit the couple's parents. The young couples are too busy, but the parents need to save face, so they would rather have a hired family visit than none at all.

Everyone groans and says, "Oh, that's awful." But then I say, Look at our culture. Some of the things we do must look just as bizarre to others. Perhaps it would seem strange to another culture that we have to pay people to listen to our problems.

Our bizarre behaviors manifest themselves in some basic disorders such as sleep deprivation, depression, loneliness, boredom, and violence.

Sleep

Here is a basic, essential, pleasant, human activity that we neglect. More than 100 million citizens are seriously sleep-deprived. One half of adults don't get enough sleep. At first this sounds like a minor problem—it's just sleep—but sleep researchers argue that sleep deprivation contributed to such disasters as the poison-gas leak at Bhopal, the Chernobyl nuclear disaster, the near-meltdown at Three Mile Island, the explosion of the *Challenger* space shuttle, and the oil spill of the Exxon *Valdez*.

But even more than accidents and injuries is the day to day feeling of exhaustion and flatness. When you don't have enough sleep, you just can't feel fully alive. Lack of sleep may contribute to another one of our problems: the prevalence of depression. We even have a new disease—chronic fatigue syndrome.

Depression

The National Institute of Mental Health says that almost 16 percent of the U.S. population is judged to be suffering from a major mental illness or substance abuse, with severe mental illness more common than cancer, diabetes, or heart disease. And these are just the people diagnosed by insurance companies as needing treatment. Many millions more are just plain depressed.

What is depression? The mental health profession defines it as feeling sad or empty, with a loss of interest or pleasure in ordinary activities, including sex. There is decreased energy, sleep disturbance, eating disturbance, feelings of hopelessness and pessimism, feelings of guilt and worthlessness, irritability, thoughts of death or suicide, chronic aches and pains. The National Institute of Mental Health says it's the way 17.6 million adults experience life. In any one year, 10 percent of our population is clinically depressed.

Since World War II, depression has increased dramatically— some say there is ten times as much depression as before the war. One indicator is the growth in the prescriptions of antidepressants like Prozac. In 1993, 5 million people in the United States were using Prozac.

The sense of the bizarre grows when we discover that Prozac is increasingly prescribed for children, even children as young as three years old. Some estimates find that since 1992, prescriptions of antidepressant drugs for children have quadrupled.

More and more, Prozac prescriptions are written for people who are suffering from what is seen as normal life stress. The symptoms include not eating or eating too much, not sleeping or over-sleeping, poor concentration or difficulty making decisions. Who doesn't identify with these? It sounds like just plain unhappiness. One survey found that 48 percent of Americans experience these symptoms.

In 1991, an ad was placed in the *Village Voice* that said, "Are you depressed? Do you suffer from fatigue? Inability to concentrate? Have trouble sleeping or eating? If so, contact . . . "

There were thousands of phone calls.

Loneliness

Depression is second cousin to loneliness. More people live alone in this country than ever before. In 1950, only 10 percent of households consisted of just one person, but by 1994, 24 percent of households had only one person—which means that 12 percent of the adult population lives alone. A 1990 Gallup poll found that more than 36 percent of Americans say they are lonely.

But it's not just living alone, it's that we don't gather together just to be together. I often ask people how much they sing. Try it.

What you'll find is that people sing, but they are almost all singing alone in their cars or their showers. And they dance alone. All by themselves in their living room. What does this mean? Here is a basic human activity that people have done throughout history as a source of joy and community, and it has almost totally disappeared from our lives.

And all of this goes against anyone's better judgment, for we know that loneliness is bad for us. Healthy people who are isolated are twice as likely to die over a ten-year period as healthy people who aren't isolated. Isolated men are four times more likely to die of all causes at any age than less isolated men. People with heart disease have a poor chance of survival if they are unmarried and don't have a confidant.

We know there should be something more. Everyone wants friends, but you hesitate to ask people over, fearing that they are too busy or that you will appear too needy. As if needing friends were some sort of a weakness.

Boredom

It's hard to get statistics on boredom because for some it's just their normal experience, so boredom manifests itself in strange ways. It shows itself in a taste for the violent or bizarre in entertainment; it shows itself in addictions. Most of all, boredom shows itself in our long hours of watching television—television that isn't even very good; it shows itself in our long hours at the mall buying junk and thinking we're participating in community because there are other shoppers walking around.

Violence

Boredom is expressed in violence. Of industrialized countries, we rank number one in murder. We're number one in murder of children, in deaths by gun, and in deaths by capital punishment. We do bizarre things like pass laws allowing people to carry concealed guns. In Texas, which has such a law, traffic altercations are deadly. Someone cuts you off in traffic, you get your gun out and shoot him.

THE PARADOX OF SUCCESS

Most people are just trying to be happy, to be successful in the only way that they know how. We do what we've learned to do, what we're expected to do, what everyone else is doing. We've been trying to get a piece of the American Dream. And what is the result? John R. O'Neil in *The Paradox of Success* tells about the lives of those at the top of corporations, the ones that are "successful." He says that under their veneer of control is depression and despair. And it's no wonder, because to get to where they are they've had to give up almost everything—time with themselves, time with friends and families, and most of all they have had to give up their values and their early dreams of making a difference in the world. In some ways that's true for the majority of people in this country.

Stress on the job is at an all-time high. One U.S. survey found that almost one-quarter of the workforce between the ages of twenty-five and forty-four suffered from stress-induced nervous strain bad enough to "diminish performance." Stress-related disorders are soon to be the most prevalent reason for claiming worker disability. Absenteeism has tripled in the last fifteen years, much of it related to stress. People report fatigue, anxiety, insomnia, headaches, dizziness, panic attacks, depression, cardiac disorders, backache, weakened immune systems, and substance abuse. About 10 percent of the workforce is addicted to drugs or alcohol.

OUR PERSONAL LIVES

We rarely put all this information together. We don't see these facts as an overarching picture. And facts are cold-blooded—they don't really tell us about real people's lives. Think about things that have happened to your friends in the last few years. How many women do you know who were diagnosed with breast cancer? How many people have you met who must isolate themselves because they cannot tolerate the toxic chemicals they are surrounded with in daily life? Who do you know whose son has a drug-abuse problem? How many of your friends were divorced this year?

THE EARTH IS DYING TOO

It is not only people who are suffering. The earth is dying. Perhaps our despair is a reflection of the dying earth. We see the link most directly in statistics on cancer: in 1900, one person out of thirty-three got cancer. Now it is one out of three.

As the outer world sickens, so does our inner world. Everything around us is dying. Global warming, the hole in the ozone layer, polluted air and water, depleted topsoil, deforestation: With the earth dying, how could we feel alive? The sicknesses of people and the planet are linked.

The tragic irony is that we can change all of this. We can quit polluting the earth, quit poisoning ourselves. We must develop a new approach to life, but first we need to understand the underlying causes of our problems.

2

THE AMERICAN NIGHTMARE

THE SELLING OF OUR SOUL

Why, in our time, have societies well endowed with industrial plenty and scientific genius turned uglier with totalitarian violence than any barbarous people? . . . Why do nihilism and neurosis brood over what we please to call the "developed" societies, taking as great a toll of human happiness as gross physical privation in the third world?

Is it not clear enough that these are the many twisted faces of despair?

—THEODORE ROSZAK

FROM THE AMERICAN DREAM TO THE AMERICAN NIGHTMARE: THE EMPTINESS OF OUR SUCCESS

We have had the greatest wealth—nothing like it ever before in human history. Why has the American Dream been transformed into the American Nightmare?

Somehow we have come to believe that happiness comes from material goods, an impressive job, or status and power.

Now, if we actually asked people if they think that being rich and successful would make them happy, they will say no. They say they know that money and all it buys is not what is important in life. But that's not the way they behave. For instance, look how the lottery affects people. Research shows that people who win the lottery are ecstatic the first week, but a year later they are not only no more happy than they were, but they are probably less happy. But, even knowing that research predicts unhappiness, most of us think that *we* would be an exception. *We* would be happier if we won the lottery—we could handle it.

Deep down, we think being rich would make us happy. It's as if we are under the spell of an evil genie. The evil genie takes the form of greed.

GREED

When asked to characterize the American people, this is the word that springs to many lips. A study done for the Merck Family Fund by the Harwood Group asked people to talk about their concerns for our country. People were profoundly worried about our country's direction, and overwhelmingly referred to the root of our problems as greed. Almost 95 percent of the respondents saw Americans as greedy, materialistic people.

But what is greed? It's revealed in the statistics on our country. Comparing the United States to the other industrial nations, this is what we find:

- We're number one in billionaires and number one in children and elderly living in poverty.

- We're number one in real wealth and number one in unequal wealth distribution.

- We're number one in big homes and number one in homelessness.

- We're number one in private consumption and last in saving.

- We're number one in executive salaries and number one in inequality of pay.

But saying that greed is the underlying cause of our problems is too simple. *Why* are we greedy? Is it just human nature? Of course greed is a part of human nature, but so is caring and generosity. What accounts for the fact that greed seems to predominate? In the last book he wrote before he died, *To Have or to Be*, Erich Fromm suggests that it is the institutions and systems of a society that create the behavior of the people. What are the institutions and systems in our society that have created such a greedy, uncaring people?

HIERARCHY/DOMINATION

Remember King of the Mountain, the game we played as kids? It was a pretty unsophisticated game. As I recall, you just ran up a little hill and tried to push off the kid standing on top. Then someone else would try to push you off. Little did we know that the game was a form of boot camp for American life.

Almost everything in American life is set up as a hierarchy: the schools, the government, the church, businesses. We think in hierarchies, placing ourselves above or below people in terms of status and behaving accordingly. The person with more status is always treated better—listened to more, deferred to more. Do you talk to your boss the same as you talk to the janitor? No. You can tell who's the boss just by watching two people talk: the boss talks more, interrupts more, tells more jokes. The subordinate just laughs and listens.

We spend most of our lives trying to get to the top of the heap. We see life as a ladder to success. We've learned that to move up the ladder, you have to knock someone else off the next rung. Life for Americans is a scramble for hierarchy and position. Higher is always better, more is always better—a prescription for greed.

When I was an administrator, I was always of two minds. I could see that the higher I moved up, the duller the job got. More long-winded meetings, less time spent in touch with students. It was a pain. But on the other hand, a little voice was always prompting me to try to advance, to strive for more money and more status. I don't think we realize the strength of that little voice that urges us to move up, to dominate.

We are caught in a vicious cycle. As we climb the ladder and spend less and less time with caring activities, we feel uncared for. As we experience this lack of caring, we turn to counterfeit activities to establish our self-worth. For instance, we become obsessed with competing and winning.

COMPETITION

King of the Mountain was pretty unsophisticated compared to the game that really prepared us to be Americans—Monopoly. In Monopoly, we learned to compete, we learned to swallow our pity for the poor person who lost all of his property. What a game! Actually, it wasn't really a game. We weren't really playing, because you didn't laugh much, and you sure learned to hate the guys who took your money.

We have an obsession with winning and achieving. What's one of the biggest insults? To call someone a loser. Why do we compete so obsessively? Is it an effort to feel valued? Now, it would be nice if we learned that we have value just because we exist. It would be wonderful if we felt that self-worth is the birthright of every human being. But that's not what happens. We learn very early that self-esteem is based on others' approval. And this approval comes only when we have won some sort of competition. When we're young it's pretty straightforward: to be a winner you need to be good in school, good at sports, prettier than other people, more popular than other people. Everything is measured in terms of who is *number one*.

We know how ugly it can get—parents yelling at Little League Games, parents pressuring their kids to take lesson after lesson. Study, practice! You won't get into Harvard! You won't get a good job!

When my kids were four and five, I took them to an Easter egg hunt held in one of our parks. That sounds like a benign community activity. But what did they do? They lined up all the kids. Told them to get ready, get set, *go!* All the kids raced off picking up the candy strewn around the grass. My kids stood there wondering what had happened. We never went again.

What kind of an Easter celebration was that? An American Easter celebration.

There's no need to talk about the cult of winning that we experience as adults. For most of us the place to win is in the workplace. The feelings are so intense, with everyone posturing and back-stabbing—all to get ahead. Not only do we work more hours, much of our nonworking hours are devoted to activities that will help us get ahead—taking courses, getting fit, networking. When people lose their jobs, they lose their self-worth because they look like losers.

Alfie Kohn, in his book *No Contest*, gives a perceptive analysis of the role that competition plays in our society. For instance, competition makes us an anxious people. Kohn quotes Rollo May as saying that competition is the primary cause of anxiety in our culture. And you can never really relax and say, Whew, that's over! There is always another contest. Once you have been the winner, others want to defeat you. And if you keep competing, it gets harder the higher you go—you face stiffer competition, and the more likely you are to lose.

The irony of all this is that winning never really gets you the caring that you need. In fact, the more successful you are, the more the resentment builds against you. We worship celebrities for about two minutes and then we turn on them. Nonetheless, people are thrilled when they get to be on television, and, as we know, they will reveal the most shameful personal secrets to have those few minutes of fame. And even the fleeting fame of media exposure doesn't bring self-esteem or caring. One man told me that his family had been featured in a *Time* magazine article—a story about how today's families are coping—and they got hate mail for two years after.

In her book *Plain and Simple*, Sue Bender describes what it was like to be at a party with her old friends after she had spent time with the Amish:

> All their energies were spent staking out territory,
> confusing what they did with who they were. . . . I knew
> that part of me would always want to be a star. But this
> never-ending pushy order would never give me what I was
> seeking. . . . No matter how much you acquired or
> accomplished, something was always missing. . . .
> Suddenly I had a vivid image of sharks all around me. I
> had been competing, without understanding how
> competitive I was, telling myself that swimming with
> sharks was normal.

So it's clear that our competitive way of life causes us to feel uncared for and causes us to be greedy, leading to depression and anxiety. Once again we have to ask if being competitive is normal. Surely people have always competed. Margaret Mead, who studied many cultures, says:

> The most basic conclusion which comes out of this
> research is that competitive and cooperative behavior on
> the part of individual members of a society is
> fundamentally conditioned by the total social emphasis of
> that society, that the goals for which individuals will work
> are culturally determined and are not the response of the
> organism to an external, culturally undefined situation.

Apparently, we are doing it to ourselves. Why?

CONSUMPTION

If people are very competitive they become more insecure and less caring toward others. As people experience an uncaring society, they look for ways to prove they are worthy. Worthiness is equated with being successful, and having a lot of material things is a sign that you are successful. Therefore, the more competitive and uncaring a society becomes, the more people will consume. It is a vicious circle.

And consumption is clearly an activity that does not lead to the sense of security and value that we are searching for—we have seen that our levels of consumption in this country are killing the planet and killing us. As we consume, we use up the earth's resources and human resources. As we consume, we are forced to work more and more. So we pollute the earth, and poison ourselves.

The New Road Map Foundation, founded by Vicki Robin, co-author with Joe Dominguez of *Your Money or Your Life*, has devoted itself to reducing consumption in this country and has unearthed some interesting statistics about our shopping behavior:

- The average time spent shopping per week is six hours. The typical household carries $8,570 of non-mortgage personal debt.

- In the last twenty years, the rise in per capita consumption in the United States has been 45 percent.

- Shopping is the most popular out of home activity.

- Over 90 percent of teenage girls say that shopping is their favorite activity.

When we use shopping as entertainment, we are taking time away from activities that *would* lead to this elusive sense of worth. We are taking time away from being with friends and family, time away from inner growth or spiritual reflection, forcing us again into the vicious cycle of competition and greed.

Where will this all stop? Everything in our society is geared to make it as easy as possible to consume. Although we had a big fracas over making it easier to register to vote, no one is worried about making it easier to consume. You don't have to *go* someplace to shop anymore. In fact, as shopping on the Internet increases, you won't even have to pick up your phone.

If we are looking at the forces in our society that make us greedy, the ease of consumption is one. But maybe you think that consumption is an individual decision, that no one is forcing us to buy. Theoretically that's true. But, when you analyze the forces driving us to consume, you realize it is a systemic problem, not just an individual failing.

MARKETING AND ADVERTISING

There is another reason we have thrown ourselves into consuming: it is because we are victims of propaganda that we are almost powerless to resist. Our materialistic way of life is shoved down our throats every minute of the day, and because we are so cut off from meeting our real needs, we are even more vulnerable to marketing's message.

And what is the message? The message is that if you want to be happy, buy something.

Advertising promotes the very thing that underlies many of our problems—materialism and greed. It tells us that the answer to feeling lonely, feeling undervalued, feeling bored is to buy something, not to change the way we are living. Instead of encouraging us to develop our inner lives, it urges us to focus on our image and appearances.

Advertisers say that they don't create desires, that they are just responding to what people want. But we all know how many times we have gone to the store and bought something we saw on TV—something we had never even known existed. And yet, we had to have it. Advertising can make something look so desirable, so exciting, that we actually feel that it will change our lives. And then we get it home and never even use it.

Advertising promotes feelings of dissatisfaction with our lives. There are no problems in those commercials. Everybody is happy, everyone is slim, their houses are clean, there is no arguing, no mess. We look around at our own lives and find them lacking. It makes us want new things, makes us dissatisfied with something old, and so we accept the planned obsolescence that is built into so many of our products and causes so much environmental degradation.

All this is not only destroying our satisfaction with ourselves and our lives, it is taking our time. It's not only shopping that takes our time, it's the commercials themselves. An average person spends about an hour a day reading, watching, or listening to television and radio commercials. By the time we are seventy-five years old, advertising will have stolen about four years of our life.

COMMERCIALISM: MONEY AND POWER CORRUPT

As human beings, we are capable of both greed and generosity—it is the institutions of a society that determine the direction we take—the institutional structures of hierarchy, competition, consumption, and advertising. But at the same time that these institutions shape our behavior, the institutions themselves are shaped by a belief system, a view of life, a system of values.

Our dominant value in this country is money and power, and money and power corrupt. The affluent life is just not good for people: affluent people are bored, looking for titillation; affluent people are worn down by a constant oversupply of stuff, of entertainment—they are satiated and desensitized. Affluent people begin to feel they have a right to abuse people and the planet.

Wise people have always said that power corrupts, and of course we see it all the time. The person with too much power becomes a bully, becomes obsessed with power. Just so, a person with too much money becomes obsessed with money. It takes over our minds. Maybe that's what has happened to us. Like weeds in the garden, the trappings of wealth have crowded out the more beautiful flowers of caring and happiness.

A NEW SYSTEM OF BELIEF

We need something to stop us. Perhaps we need a vision of life that will bring us the inspiration to change our institutions. Some are suggesting that we need a whole new consciousness, a whole new way of looking at life. With a new vision we can begin to create institutions that will help us become generous, caring people instead of greedy, uncaring people. We need a system of belief that will shape our institutions, bringing them under control. People are finding that vision in the philosophy of voluntary simplicity.

3

SAVING OUR SOULS

AWAKENING TO A NEW VISION

Nothing less, I think, than that we should undertake to repeal urban-industrialism as the world's dominant style of life. We should do this, not in a spirit of grim sacrifice, but in the conviction that the reality we want most to reside in lies beyond the artificial environment.

—THEODORE ROSZAK

RECLAIMING THE SACREDNESS OF LIFE

When I think of modern life, the phrase that comes to me is that "Nothing is sacred." Everything is for sale. I'm beginning to hear it a lot. For instance, there's the joke about the devil and the Hollywood agent. The devil tells the agent that he can get him any star he wants—Madonna, Paul Newman, Sharon Stone, anyone—the only thing he asks in return is the agent's soul. "What's the catch?" responds the agent.

Are we all prostitutes, willing to sell ourselves? I hate it when I see someone I have respected on a commercial. Who will sell out next? Will I? Will everyone?

THE MATERIALISTIC WORLDVIEW

Our extreme consumption is the expression of a materialistic philosophy of life, but this has not always been the philosophy people have lived by. For thousands of years another, more joyful, philosophy existed, as Carolyn Merchant explains in her book *Radical*

Ecology. She describes how ancient cultures, including the native peoples of America, saw the earth as a mother—alive, active, and responsive to human action. The Greeks and the Renaissance Europeans, too, saw the earth as a nurturing mother, the cosmos as a living organism, with a body, soul, and spirit. The relationship between most peoples and the earth was an I-thou ethic. When people dammed a brook or cut a tree, they thanked the spirit of the earth.

But all that has changed.

We replaced the organic view with the view that nature was dead, to be used by humans however they wanted. In the seventeenth century, the modern science of experimentation and manipulation emerged, and we began to see life in terms of the newly emerging machine. The scientific and industrial revolutions were underway.

AN ECOCENTRIC WORLDVIEW

Carolyn Merchant suggests that we need to move from an egocentric ethic grounded in the mechanistic world view to an ecocentric ethic that values people and the planet. Our current egocentric ethic springs from a mechanistic view of the world—if the world is lifeless matter, it's logical to do with it what we want.

An ecocentric ethic is rooted in a holistic metaphysics in which everything is connected to everything else. A change in one part will cause a change in another part. There is a unity of humans and non-human nature. Adopting such an ethic, one that values nature, can change the way we live. Everything we do, then, must take into account its affect on people *and* the planet.

Indian philosopher Eknath Easwaran explores the same idea in *The Compassionate Universe:*

> My grandmother lived in a universe filled with life. It was impossible for her to conceive of any creature—even the smallest insect, let alone a human being—as insignificant.

In every leaf, flower, animal, and star she saw the
expression of a compassionate universe, whose laws were
not competition and survival of the fittest but cooperation,
artistry, and thrift . . . In our way of life, our farming, our
business and barter, our friendships, we were guided by
her ideal of an individual life rooted in continuous
harmony with life as a whole.

VOLUNTARY SIMPLICITY

The day to day expression of the ecocentric ethic is the life of voluntary simplicity. The life of voluntary simplicity is a life lived consciously, a decision to live in harmony with life, to show reverence
for life, to sustain life. It is a life of creativity and celebration, a life
of community and participatory democracy, and a life in touch with
nature and the universal life force. It is a life that has soul, it is a life
that allows the individual's soul to awaken.

PART 2

GETTING CLEAR

CLEARING AWAY THE BRAMBLES

Whenever we start a new project, we clear things away first. There is a feeling that as we clear out the space around us, space within will open up.

So, in beginning this quest to simplify our lives, we begin by getting rid of the chaos and the clutter. Think of it as a sort of hacking away the brambles so that we can seek the trail head.

To develop our vision of simplicity, a vision of living consciously, we must take a look at what gets in our way of living fully—all the things we think we have to do, all the stuff we have accumulated, all the junk we buy.

Only then will we be able to seek new trails.

4

SEEING CLEARLY

A VISION OF VOLUNTARY SIMPLICITY

Most of the luxuries, and many of the so-called
comforts of life, are not only not indispensable, but
positive hindrances to the elevation of mankind. With
respect to luxuries and comforts, the wisest have ever
lived a more simple and meager life than the poor.

—HENRY DAVID THOREAU

A VISION

I saw a picture in the paper one day of an Amish family in a one-horse open sleigh. I felt so envious. I wanted that simple feeling of joy. Being outside, being in the snow, being with people I loved. Going home to a community that valued me.

Did they appreciate the freedom I was envious of? What were they thinking about? Were they dreading going home, facing all the things they needed to do, the people that they had to deal with? Whenever I come home from a trip, my stomach knots up when I walk up to the front door. I know that there will be mountains of mail to sift through, dozens of calls on voice mail to listen to.

I know I can't be Amish. But I can begin to try to explore the values of voluntary simplicity that they live by. What are those values? What is the vision of voluntary simplicity?

THOREAU

I first encountered the philosophy of voluntary simplicity when I was sixteen, sitting in Miss Newell's English class. That was the year

I read the words that still stir me: "I went to the woods because I wished to live deliberately, to front only the essential facts of life, and see if I could not learn what it had to teach, and not, when I came to die, discover that I had not lived."

For me, in this passage from *Walden*, Henry David Thoreau was defining voluntary simplicity. Let's take it phrase by phrase.

"I went to the woods": we may not have a cabin in the woods, but we need some way to withdraw, at least in little ways. It might mean turning off the television, getting up early in the morning—somehow separating ourselves from our day-to-day lives. We need some time alone, away from the frenzy of everyday life.

"Because I wished to live deliberately": to live deliberately is to live consciously—we need to think through the consequences of our actions, to ask how they will affect our lives and how they will affect the earth. We have to question everything we do. Why are we doing it? Does it need to be done? How does it affect the well being of people and the planet.

We learn to pay attention to how we feel, to our inner source of knowledge, asking ourselves if we really like our profession or are we just in it for the money. Are we really fond of the person we married, or did we only marry to make our parents happy? Do we really like our house, or did we only buy it for the status? Living consciously means asking all of these questions. It means living our own life, discovering who we are and how we want to live.

"To front only the essential facts of life": in living deliberately and consciously, we focus on the essential facts of life. We quit worrying about the inessential things like our clothes, our hair, our golf game, our next promotion. We examine the essential things: how much time we are spending with our friends, how we are contributing to the greater good.

"And see if I could not learn what it had to teach": instead of just learning from books, we learn from our own life experiences. We look at the turning points in our lives and ask ourselves what we learned from them. What did we learn when our husband left us?

When we lost our job? When we took that trip to Europe? We look at the experiences that changed our lives and ask what they tell us about success and failure.

"And not, when I came to die, discover that I had not lived": this is the sentence that still moves me. This is it. This is the core of voluntary simplicity. We are trying to find a way to live that helps us become fully alive. We are trying to discover and remove the things that are deadening, that cause us to escape to drugs and to shopping and to television, all the things that numb us and put us asleep.

QUAKERS

Later, in college, I discovered the Quakers, the Society of Friends. At first I was a little wary. Who were these people whose worship service consisted of sitting in silence, with only the periodic voice of someone moved to speak? Over time, though, I came to understand and love their ideas, their commitment to following their inner light, looking within to discover value and meaning. It was a Quaker, Richard Gregg, who first used the phrase voluntary simplicity. In his words, "voluntary simplicity involves both inner and outer condition. It means . . . sincerity and honesty within, as well as avoidance of exterior clutter. . . . The degree of simplification is a matter for each individual to settle for himself."

DUANE ELGIN

My next encounter with simplicity was in Duane Elgin's book *Voluntary Simplicity*. I can remember standing in a book store in 1981, looking at the book, thinking that here was a book that would change my life. His phrase, living a life that was "outwardly simple and inwardly rich," caught me the way Thoreau's words did. Elgin sees it as a movement that leads people from a life of materialism to a life of inner joy. Giving up our obsession with consumption will give us time to explore our inner potential.

Voluntary simplicity, for people like Thoreau, Gregg, and Elgin, always involves both our outer lives and our inner lives, always involves changing our lives so that we live more fully and joyfully.

THE COMMON PERSON'S DEFINITION

But we need not rely only on these profound thinkers to understand simplicity. Central to this movement is the voice of the common, ordinary person. Part of living simply is consulting your own wisdom, listening to your own inner voice. So let us listen to the words of simplicity circle members as they define voluntary simplicity. Their thoughtfulness in defining voluntary simplicity confirms my belief that it is the common person's wisdom that will save us.

Time

The first thing that brings people to simplicity circles is their feeling that they have no time.

I want to break free from my daily routine. I'm swept away by minutia.

I want more time for reflection, more time to be human.

I want to live at a slower pace. I quit management to become a carpenter and I've never been happier in my life. Before I was buying into the bullshit—it hooked me pretty bad.

Freedom

But then, you begin to notice that it is something more than time. It is a concern that you get to choose how you spend your time, a concern that someone else is controlling you. It's a concern for freedom.

I want to live my own life, not a life lived to someone else's agenda.

I want to live simply so that no one can own me.

I want to figure out what is really important.

Purpose

Part of this freedom is having a life of meaning, feeling that the way you live makes a difference.

For me, voluntary simplicity is living life with purpose. I used to be in an administrative position in nursing. It was too many hours and I wanted to go back to doing what I love, which is direct care of the patients.

It is choosing where to put my energy, living my values, making conscious decisions. Valuing the nonmaterial and the nonproductive parts of life.

What I used to think was the answer to happiness turned out not to be true. I got a good job, and planned to say with the job until I retired and then I would do what I wanted. But my brother died from AIDS and now I see life differently. My job brought me no passion, and I believe we all have something to offer and it is my responsibility to find out what that is, so I'm going back to school. Not having any money doesn't scare me.

Identity

There's a hunger to be who you are, to develop your authentic self.

Voluntary simplicity means to live authentically—living my values, speaking my truths, even if I look crazy. It is an expression of who I am: my values, inner self. It is to resist pressures from outside and choose what reflects me.

I want to bring my choices in line with my values. Voluntary simplicity is a process of figuring out what is important to you and your family, and figuring out how to go against the grain.

Environment

When people realize the connection between their lifestyle and the environment, they are committed to living more lightly. But some come to the movement because this is their primary concern.

It is approaching life in a thoughtful manner with as little impact on the earth as possible.

I'm interested in sustainability, the preservation of our nonrenewable resources. It is part of my spiritual path. The potential for spiritual growth is wide open. I used to work at Boeing in a high-stress job managing military proposals. I rationalized for a long time. Finally I worked on a proposal for nuclear warheads. That precipitated a 'dark night of the soul.' I couldn't go on. I was sinking fast into quicksand, so I took a medical leave.

After I came back from the leave, I saw a picture of Gandhi and his belongings. There were about four things—a book, his glasses, a fountain pen, and his sandals . . . something like that. I couldn't believe it.

We moved to an island where we have a view of water and the mountains that gives me 'a peace that passes understanding.' At first we just went on the weekends. Then I was in a car accident, a difficult gift. Without it, though, I would have continued in technical writing and that is not in tune with my soul.

The accident forced me to step back and to consider my life—how I will heal. It has been an incredible journey. I focus on bringing beauty into our lives and on healing rather than achievement.

Clutter and Consumption

A lot of people just feel overwhelmed with junk in their lives. They feel they can't get started on any other changes until they can clear things out.

I just moved to a smaller house so I'm getting rid of stuff and asking about each item—is it enriching my life or cluttering my life? It's so freeing to cut back. I want to free up more money, time, and emotional energy. I try to get rid of things that don't fit me, that don't reflect me. I think about how they make me feel.

To me, voluntary simplicity is getting to the essence of things. . . . You can do things that you love, but it grows and you forget what you loved about it.

I think of voluntary simplicity as stepping off the high consumer path. Even though I don't consume much, compared to the rest of the world, I am a high consumer.

Money

Although saving money isn't the primary motivation for most, people find that they need the support of the philosophy of simplicity if they are going to be able to live on less.

I'm in the third year of a three-year debt-reduction process. I didn't believe I could do it, but I am. I'm trying to let go of commitments that are not fulfilling to me, things that drain instead of give me energy. I want to work to build community.

Voluntary simplicity is coming to terms with 'what is enough,' deciding what will make me happy. I want to explore who I am beyond my career.

Moving to the Country

Some just think that they can no longer live simply when they live in the city, so they focus on connecting with others who are moving to the country.

We're moving to an island and doing more simple things for pleasure, like sitting around a fire, talking and laughing. The city seems to suck you up.

Mental Health

Some feel they are being driven crazy by our lifestyle and that they have no choice but to change.

I made a major change five years ago. I was a manager in a medical field and felt I would go crazy if I didn't leave, but I was afraid I wouldn't survive. I went into nonprofit management and I have survived. I've been a single parent and now my son is eighteen. I can finally stop just surviving and think about who I am and what I want to do. I want to have more options so I don't have to work full-time.

I want to figure out what keeps me going, what keeps me clicking. Six years ago I lost my job, even though I was doing a good job and working hard, and I was devastated. I realized I could not identify myself with my job. I'm a nurse, but I want to change to something that doesn't suck so much energy out of me.

Health

Many are forced to look at living more simply when they find their health is affected.

I want my health and time. I quit my teaching job two years ago because it was ruining my health. To me, voluntary simplicity is moment by moment awareness, and it includes my spiritual life. There is so much beauty around us.

Fulfillment

What everyone is ultimately talking about is finding a life of fulfillment. Living consciously, choosing their lives, feeling grateful for what they have, being able to sit back and feel that they have found the good life.

It is wanting what I have, feeling grateful and content.

Voluntary simplicity is a distilling process that goes on continually. I'm trying to get to the essence of what I choose. I have cut back to working three days a week and I'm using my time to pursue my passion.

When I went to Africa, all the women were beautiful. They were smiling all of the time, and I realized our faces are just pinched. I want to smile more.

Nurturing my soul, living purposefully, eliminating distractions, pollutions (visual, sound), having my real needs met, enjoying beauty, pleasing myself, meeting my own standards, making life whole again.

THE NEXT STEP

So there you are. So many different approaches to voluntary simplicity; so many heartfelt comments. But no one can completely define voluntary simplicity because it is something that each one of us must do for ourselves. We can see, though, that the core of voluntary simplicity is trying to answer that age-old question: How shall I live? What will make me happy? What is the good life?

But defining voluntary simplicity is only a first step. Let's now turn to the ways we can put the theories into practice.

5

CLEARING SPACE

LIVING CONSCIOUSLY

Many of them had a better time than they ever had in their lives because they were discovering the new freedom—the less you need, the freer you become.
—E. F. Schumacher

When was the last time you got in your car, started out for one destination and ended up somewhere else? You were on your way to a movie, but your car started heading toward work. We know we're on automatic pilot when we do that. But how much do we do that in the rest of our lives? How much do we just go through our days making the same turns, reacting the same way?

When you live your life on automatic, you fall victim to Thoreau's fear, expressed his words "and not, when I came to die, discover that I had not lived." By living automatically, you miss your life. It goes by without you.

When I was a junior in high school, we read Thornton Wilder's *Our Town*, where the young mother dies and gets to come back, unobserved by others, to look at her life one last time. It's almost too painful to read. She feels so acutely how little she appreciated her day to day life, how much she took her life for granted.

But we all do that. It isn't until something happens—we get sick, a loved one dies—that we notice what we had. How can we live with more awareness ? Setting out on our path to live more simply involves not only the big questions we've been discussing but also the little day to day things—the TV you watch, the clutter on your desk, the errands you run. You need to look at it all. Do they reflect conscious choices?

A lot of people have read *Your Money or Your Life*, the book by Joe Dominguez and Vicki Robin that helps you reduce your spending. The authors suggest that you start writing down everything that you buy and then take a look at where your money is going and decide if you want to keep spending it that way.

Maybe we should do the same for our time. Maybe we should keep a little notebook and, every hour, take note of what we're doing and how we're feeling. Maybe we should sit down at the end of the day and reconstruct our day—see what we did and how we felt. Ask ourselves how often we were feeling relaxed and peaceful and enjoying ourselves, or how often we were feeling rushed and anxious and irritated. The first step in any kind of change is getting a realistic picture of what is really going on.

GETTING STARTED

You start by looking at what you are doing, and asking yourself what the consequences of your activities are—for both yourself and the earth. Ernest Callenbach, author of *Ecotopia* shows how interwoven everything is. He talks about what he calls a *green triangle,* and he shows how almost every change you make to save money will also improve your health and help save the environment. For instance, if you drive less to save money, your health improves by walking or biking; and since you pollute less, it helps the environment.

Most of us hop in the car without thinking. We need something, so we drive to a store and buy it. When you begin to live consciously you ask yourself if you really need the item or if you can get along without it or use something else. After the first impulse to *buy* passes, you may find that you don't want the thing after all. You've saved yourself time, money, and polluted less. You are beginning to live consciously.

You begin to do this with everything. Do I really need to do this? Do I really want to spend time with this person? Do I really want to work for a promotion? You may be wondering if this really simplifies life. Be aware, we're not talking about efficiency or convenience. Sometimes living simply takes longer. We are talking about our quality of life—whether it brings joy and serenity rather than frustration and aggravation. Whether it brings a sense of congruence or fragmentation. But while simplicity may be more complex, it shouldn't be more complicated. Something that is complicated is confusing; something that is complex is challenging. A life of simplicity is complex and challenging.

THE BIG QUESTIONS

In learning to feel fully alive, you evaluate your activities in terms of energy: Does something drain your energy, or boost your energy? Does it give you a sense of aliveness or a sense of deadness? Years ago I remember reading Alan Lakein's *How to Get Control of Your Time and Your Life,* one of the only helpful time management books I ever read. He talked about prioritizing your goals into A, B, and C—nothing unusual in that, it's the same sort of thing that everyone says. What I liked about him was what he said next. After figuring out what your Cs are—the things that drain your energy—you try to get out of doing them as long as you can. You learn to ask yourself just how important is this, anyway, in the great scheme of things.

Often your Cs are the things that you are doing unconsciously: mindless shopping, driving around doing errands, spending time with people you don't really like. You are doing them because everyone else is doing them or because someone else is pressuring you. For instance, one of my Cs is cleaning my car. There was always a nagging voice (usually my husband's) telling me to clean up the car. But when I read Lakein, I quit feeling guilty. It was just too draining for me to try to clean the car every week, so I put it off as long as I could—until I couldn't stand it any more. Then I cleaned it, grateful for all the time I had saved.

So you start looking at your time carefully, living consciously, *choosing* the things that you do. What you discover is that the things that drain your energy also drain the earth's energy. Washing my car less often meant using less soap and water, so I saved not only my time, but the planet's resources.

REDUCING CLUTTER

At the beginning of each study circle, we always talk about why people are drawn to voluntary simplicity. And the answer often is: I want to get rid of my clutter. We want to get rid of the stacks of mail we plan to read someday, the pile of magazines we mean to get through, the drawers that have deteriorated to a collection of junk that we want to sort. How do you get rid of clutter?

Now, the real answer to clutter is to bring less stuff into our houses, but it's also questioning society's standards. In our culture, a person who can keep their space organized is seen as superior to the person who can't. (No one ever apologizes because their house is too neat.) If you really think about it, maybe the piles of stuff don't really bother you, and you only think you *should* be bothered, that you *should* be neat like others. Some people are just naturally neat, and they have no idea what the fuss is. They actually *like* to spend time organizing their desks and cupboards. But the people who get no pleasure from organizing things just can't be expected to have a totally neat space. Trying to do that just puts too much drain on their energy.

So part of dealing with clutter is recognizing who you really are. We are not all logical and orderly. In fact, one book on organizing clutter is particularly helpful because it recognizes the fact that people *are* different. *Organizing for the Creative Person* says that things that work for the orderly person will *not* work for the disorderly—or the *creative*, as authors Dorothy Lehmkuhl and Dolores Cotter Lamping call them. For example, drawers and file cabinets just don't work for *creative* people. These people need hooks and open shelves. They need to keep things in their sight or sooner or later, every drawer becomes a junk drawer.

Maybe the answer to your worry about clutter, then, is a question of self-knowledge. But usually the real problem is that we just have too much stuff to keep organized, so we have to figure out how to reduce what we have.

Get Rid of Things

Getting rid of things may be one of the most liberating things you can do. But a lot of people just can't decide what to get rid of. Let peace of mind be your guide. When you clear things out, ask if something makes you feel more alive and peaceful or confused and overwhelmed. You'll keep some things that seemingly have no use—maybe they will remind you of a happy time in your past. I will always keep things that my mother gave to me before she died. But I have finally decided that I must get rid of a lot of books—I have so many that I can't find the right book when I need it.

Anyone who has ever cleaned out a closet and sent stuff to Goodwill knows how liberating it is. You feel lighter, your mind feels clearer. You can have a garage sale. If the thought of spending time on a garage sale is as abhorrent as it was to me, have someone else do it and give them a percentage of the profit. Or do it with your neighbors—at least it will be more fun. Anything that is drudgery is more fun when you do it with others.

Clearing out clothes is a good thing to discuss in the study circle. People have a lot of ideas. Some people sell their clothes at flea markets. Some people arrange their own bartering, with everyone bringing clothes one evening and exchanging them with each other.

Maybe we should set up more "free" boxes as they do at Evergreen State College in Washington, one of the colleges that still nurtures the alternative spirit of the sixties. When you're tired of your clothes, you put them in the box and take whatever you want. It's a great way to meet people. You see someone walking by and you stop them and say, "That used to be my blouse!"

Don't Collect Stuff

Of course, the only thing that works is just not bringing stuff into the house in the first place. It means not picking up free information; it means not getting things "just in case" you might need them (because you'll never find them); it means not buying huge amounts of something just because it was on discount (I always worried that I would buy lots of toilet paper and then I would die and that would be all my family would have to remember me by). It means not buying little toys that your dog will surely ignore. It means not buying books off of the remainder table. It means renting ski equipment until you're sure you'll really love skiing.

People develop little rules for themselves—like every time they buy something, they have to get rid of something. Others put things in a box in the basement with the date on it. If after one year you have forgotten what was in the box, give it away without opening it. Some have a free garage sale—putting stuff out and inviting people to take it.

Finally, getting rid of clutter can be a form of self-discovery, of admitting to yourself who you really are and what you are really going to do. For years I had an exercycle in our bedroom—I usually just hung clothes on it. Every so often I would put it in the basement and then bring it back up again, thinking that I would really start using it. Getting rid of it was like a statement of freedom, really admitting that I wasn't going to use it. I don't really believe in exercycles anyway. If we're going to ride a bike, it should be a real one, outside.

DEVELOPING OUR OWN STANDARDS

Sometimes you reduce the clutter in your daily activities by clarifying your own standards. Are your housekeeping standards *your* standards, or your mother's, or the standards of *House Beautiful*?

Housekeeping

Getting beyond peer pressure is hard, particularly for women and their housekeeping. So often we're judged by what our house looks like. No one comes into a messy house and blames the husband.

In the seventies when women still had time to clean their houses, I used to give speeches in which I exhorted women to consider how much time they spent on housekeeping, and suggested that they cut back and do more important things. I encouraged them to ask themselves if they really needed to fold their clothes, when leaving them in a hamper in the closet seemed good enough. Or, did they really need to change their sheets every week as our mothers did? Although I considered these tips good advice, I quit using them when someone came up to me in a restaurant once and asked me if I was the woman who never washed her sheets!

Our housekeeping standards are created, in part, by the commercials on TV. Analyze the ads. Watch how they cleverly instill guilt in us for the way our houses look. And many of the products that they want us to buy are toxic for us and for the environment. And they're expensive. There are so many unnecessary cleaning products—you can use vinegar and baking soda for just about everything. The housekeeping standards we see on television are not only robbing us of our time, they are increasing our consumption, using up resources, polluting the environment.

We all love an attractive, comfortable home, but we should define, for ourselves, what that means.

Entertaining

I've changed my standards on entertaining, too. In the past, when people invited us over for elaborate dinners, my heart would sink because I would think, I can't have them back. It would kill me to try anything, so when we made new friends, I would have them over *first* so that I could set a really low standard.

I finally started having potlucks. At first I felt a little bad: What would people think? Would they see me as lazy, as a slacker? Then I realized that most of my friends were fully aware of the fact that I wasn't much of a cook, and they would probably *rather* bring the food. I discovered that there was a different atmosphere when people brought things. They busied themselves with their dishes; they had something to talk about—everything was much more informal and relaxed.

For a lot of us, relaxing our standards means we're more likely to have people over, but there are also people who love cooking and entertaining. If it's not a drudgery, keep doing it. Again, you choose.

LEARNING TO SAY NO

Learning to say no will simplify your life. We all want to be responsible citizens, to be involved in community activities, but we need to get out of some of the things that drain our energy.

I've always liked the story of Peace Pilgrim, the woman who, from the 1950s to the 1980s, walked back and forth across the country, walking for peace. She had only a comb, a pencil and paper, and a toothbrush. She never took any money and just waited till people offered her food or shelter. Her advice was, If you're feeling overwhelmed, you're doing too much.

When people ask me to do something, I try never to give an answer immediately, because my impulse is always to say yes—so many things sound interesting. I've learned to tell people that I will get back to them. Then, I wait a little while for my enthusiasm to subside into a more realistic response, and ask myself if I really want to do it. What will be the consequences if I say no?

If I am trying to talk myself into doing something, I've learned that's a sign to say no, because in the end I usually find a way to worm out of it. So, I call the people back up and tell them that I won't be available, that I will be busy, or just that I have other plans. None of those is really a lie. I do have plans, even if they are only to sit and do nothing.

CHANGING YOUR MIND

But most of the time we fail and agree to do things we later regret. Change your mind! That sounds horrible to most of us—we're taught not to be "quitters." I remember once hearing my husband talking to our daughter on the phone. She was calling from college, and I heard him say to her, "No, Rebecca, your mother and I never dropped any classes."

I looked at him with horror, and said, "Give me that phone!" I proceeded to tell Rebecca that I dropped out of tons of classes after finding that they were just too boring or that I didn't like them, and I eventually got my doctorate. She dropped the class she didn't like and she finished her degree, too.

EVALUATING THE PEOPLE YOU SPEND TIME WITH

Sometimes it's the people who we spend time with who drain us. Think about it. Do the people you spend time with make you blossom or shrivel up? No matter how good your self-esteem is, when you spend time with people who put you down, who ignore you, or just don't listen to you, you end up feeling bad. And some people can do it in such a subtle way that you're not really aware of what's happening. All you know is that you start stammering and getting confused when you talk to them. Around these people you feel like you have nothing to say, that you're an incredibly dull person.

Then, there are others who make you blossom. When you are around them you become witty and clever and you end up saying really perceptive things. So, as much as you can, choose your friends consciously. Some friends once told me that they were prioritizing their friends and crossing people off their list. "However," they said, "you're still on the list." I don't recommend their methods, but nonetheless, it's the sort of thing that must be done.

SPENDING LESS TIME ON APPEARANCE

For many of us, the competition for status also extends to our appearance and keeping up can drain us of time and money. For instance, take grooming: my philosophy has always been to do as little as possible, but enough to avoid comment.

Being involved in the voluntary simplicity movement is certainly helpful in this regard. No one has very high standards for you—you could wear just a few different outfits over and over and everyone would think you are making a statement, not being lazy.

Keeping up with fashion drains your time and money. Why not try to dress in a way that reveals your true self? Most people are much more comfortable around people who don't look absolutely perfect, anyway.

CUTTING BACK ON TIME WASTERS

Only you can decide what actually wastes your time, but there are a few things—like making too many phone calls or watching too much TV—that are on everyone's list. Sometimes we do these things only because it never occurred to us that there was an alternative.

Answering the Phone

I once spent some time writing in a cabin in the woods with no phone, and it was incredible how much more I could concentrate. Even though I rarely answer the phone at home, the ringing is a distraction. You begin to wonder just how much we put up with what we have always accepted as normal.

Now I have begun turning the ringer off as well, but the problem still arises: Should I return all the phone messages that I get? I have found that I just cannot do it.

Watching Television

When I wake up in the morning, I like to lie in bed thinking through the day. One morning, I realized that I was thinking about the television program that I had watched the night before. It wasn't a violent or bad program, just a standard sitcom. But I realized that I didn't want to spend time thinking about that television program, thinking about these people who didn't really matter, and I wondered what it was like for the person who had watched something violent, or the person who watched TV all of the time. What did they have running through their minds?

I've always had a TV and I have never appreciated the people who made a point of saying that they *never* watched TV. When you would ask, "Did you see so and so on television?" they could just say "No." But they almost always say, "We don't watch TV," making you feel shallow and silly.

So I'm not totally denouncing television, although the more I think about how it has affected American life the more I think we would be better off without it. Nonetheless, it's here, so how do we deal with it. You have to monitor your television watching. Only watch the programs that totally absorb you. Make it hard to watch by putting it in an out of the way place—one woman put her television in the closet and it was such a chore to get it out that the family hardly watched it at all.

Television, of course, does much more than just waste your time. It's forming your mind, making you see life the way the advertisers see it. It is deadening your perceptions, making life seem all shiny and superficial. One night I realized just how strong an anesthetic it is—literally. My husband had had his wisdom tooth out and didn't want to take pain killers, but watching TV seemed to help!

Reducing your work week will help you cut back on television. We often watch TV because we're just exhausted and not fit for anything else. Japan is the only country who works more than we do and it is the only country that watches as much television. There is a high correlation between long work hours and excessive TV watching. You're just not fit to do anything else.

Cooking

For many people, a simpler life means cooking at home. But once again, when I ask myself how I feel about what I'm doing, I realize I'm always crabby when we make dinner at home. Now, when our kids were young, that was different. It was something we could all do together—the preparation, the eating, the cleaning. Doing things together creates a natural setting for conversation.

But now that our kids no longer live at home, I would much rather be sitting with my husband in a neighborhood cafe having dinner—meeting neighbors, reading, enjoying the feeling of community.

So my conscious choice is to do less cooking and eat out more often. Now some of you are thinking, you could save so much money at home. But living simply isn't just about saving money. That's only one factor. As we will see later, living more simply also involves building community, and for me, eating in neighborhood restaurants helps build community.

I finally concluded, though, that eating out probably does save me money. When my husband and I cook at home we are just plain irritable. I figure that eating out saves on marriage counseling, and it's certainly cheaper than a divorce.

But of course, a lot of people like cooking or have other reasons for not eating out. Once again, you must evaluate your own time and decide what are time wasters for you, regardless of what others do.

Observing the Holidays and Gift Giving

We usually observe holidays and birthdays in the manner we've always done. We don't think about it much. Now, preserving tradition can be very nice. We remember when we were kids, getting up on Christmas morning, coming out to see all of the presents under the tree. So we want to do that for our kids, too. Partly for them, and partly for ourselves. But I bet if we were really to look at what was in those piles of presents in the past, there weren't as many as we remember. And those that were there nurtured our creativity more. There were books and blocks and dolls and cars, and probably not much more. What we give today is largely the result of the pressure of TV commercials. We just give too much stuff.

Think it through. Most of us have enough stuff. And buying gifts is so traumatic. I remember the year I looked in the bottom drawer of my father's dresser and found almost all the Christmas presents I had ever bought him. That's all he could think to do with them.

When I have to buy gifts for Christmas, I'm just not filled with the joy of giving. I'm always worried that the presents aren't right, that no one will like them. They always seem either too cheap or too expensive. Opening the gifts at my house is usually accompanied by some sort of apology.

So I've always dreaded buying gifts. But now that I understand the relationship between consumerism and the destruction of the planet, things have become more clear. Buying a worthless present that costs too much, that no one will like, and that degrades the environment, is just not something I'm willing to do anymore.

It's not easy to make changes in gift giving. People come to expect you to do certain things, particularly your kids. It may mean buying fewer gifts, buying gifts that have a low environmental impact, making your gifts, buying things used, and on and on. Just talk to your family and friends about it. They might feel relieved that they don't have to keep up traditions that have become burdens. Part of living consciously is talking with others about your decisions.

Everyone has stories about ways they have cut back, and it's always a fun thing to discuss with study circle members. Here are a few of the things simplicity circle members have done.

SIMPLICITY CIRCLE MEMBERS' EXPERIENCES

I read fewer things in the newspaper that I'm not really interested in.

I crossed things off my list that I haven't done.

I quit going to Costco. I always just brought home too much stuff.

I cut back on cigarettes, carpooled to the bar, and bought pitchers instead of pints of beer.

My son needed a coat and I called the woman next door who had an older boy and asked her if he had any coat that he had outgrown. She was happy to give me his.

I share a newspaper with a neighbor who is eighty-two. She gives it to me and then I put it in the recycling.

I co-own a van and then loan it out to other people.

At work I'm not sending out so much on e-mail to everyone. Each message takes maybe ten seconds to read and if you count that up, it's a lot of time.

I try cutting as many things as I can in half. I eat half of what I used to eat, spend half of what I used to spend, try to use half of the resources I used to use. It becomes a challenging game.

A NEW APPROACH TO LIFE

These simplicity circle members haven't necessarily done anything earth-shaking, but they have begun to clear a space in their lives. Life seems less overwhelming and chaotic. When you begin to live consciously, you not only begin to enjoy life more, you begin to save money. Let's look at how we can reduce our consumption.

6

GETTING CLEAR

TRANSFORMING CONSUMPTION

> Most of the luxuries, and many of the so-called
> comforts of life, are not only not indispensable, but
> positive hindrances to the elevation of mankind. With
> respect to luxuries and comforts, the wisest have even
> lived a more simple and meagre life than the poor.
> —HENRY DAVID THOREAU

When my kids were little we bought a yellow rubber boat that would hold four people, and we planned to used it on the nearby lake. We used it twice. The kids had a great time, but we never did it again. We stored it next to the Ping-Pong table and the croquet set that we hardly ever used. Those were next to the stationary bicycle.

I'm not sure exactly where the greater problem lay: the fact that we didn't have time to use those things or the fact that we thought we needed to buy something for the family to have fun.

But, in fact, buying something is the answer to almost everything in this society. If we want to look better, we buy something; if we have a pain, we buy something; if we can't sleep, we buy something; if we want to have fun, we buy something; if we want to get more fit, we buy something. We can always buy something for anything at all.

So, as we begin to get clear in our lives, we have to start by reducing our consumption. More than almost anything else, consumerism gets in our way as we try to live fully, as we try to live in harmony with nature.

It doesn't work to simply deny yourself things. It's like going on a diet—sooner or later your system starts to rebel, and, as with diets, you gorge yourself. We have to understand *why* we need to reduce consumption first.

WHY REDUCE CONSUMPTION?

Consumerism destroys nature. As William Wordsworth wrote, "Getting and spending, we lay waste our powers: Little we see in Nature that is ours."

Many experts give us only thirty to forty years before we reach the point at which our damage to the environment becomes irreparable. Much of this damage is the result of the things we buy. The production of every single product means we have used up some of the earth. We can see it by taking a look at something as mundane as a hamburger. The *Use Less Stuff Report* takes us step by step: first, the bun. It's made of flour, which starts out as a grain, which is grown with water, fertilizer, pesticides, herbicides, and sometimes fungicides. When the seed is sown and the grain harvested, farmers use tractors and threshers and combines, which are made out of metal (which has its own production process) and use lots of oil. Using oil, of course, uses up a finite resource and pollutes the air with carbon dioxide, a greenhouse gas which causes global warming.

Then the grain is transported, sorted, milled, stored, and sent to bakeries. The buns are wrapped in plastic and shipped to stores. Every step burns fuel and produces pollution.

We haven't even reached the beef! Once again, we start with grain for feed. Then lots of water, until the cow is big enough to be shipped off to the stockyard and then to the processing plant where it is slaughtered, packaged, and shipped to warehouses in refrigerator cars and trucks.

At the warehouse, the meat is ground into patties, frozen, and stored. Then it's shipped in freezer trucks to restaurants where it's kept cold until ready to cook, using more energy. Each step uses up resources, particularly oil. And we haven't talked about cutting down the rain forests in order to graze cattle, which further produces global warming.

For one little hamburger are we willing to bring ourselves closer to a barren planet? Global warming means drastic shifts in climate, with hot places like the Midwest turning into deserts. It means the flooding of sea coast towns as the oceans rise, and the drying up of water sources. Air pollution means plants die, people die.

How can we save the earth? The fate of the environment depends on the directions of technology, population, and consumption. We need more efficient technology, like solar heating and electric cars, and we need to reduce the birthrate. Until recently, people had assumed that those two were enough. Now we know that it is just as important to reduce the rate of consumption by major industrial countries. For instance, we have more cars, we drive more, we have bigger houses, we have more air-conditioning, we fly more, we eat higher off the food chain. The industrialized fourth of the world uses fifteen times as much paper, ten times as much steel, and twelve times as much fuel as the rest of the world. American houses are twice as big as they were forty-five years ago; we have more shopping centers than high schools; we drink more soft drinks than tap water. In our time-starved lives we turn to environmentally expensive conveniences: prepared foods, disposables, clothes dryers, and kitchen appliances. We're using up nature.

Shopping Cuts Us Off from Nature

Shopping harms nature both directly and indirectly. When we shop, we not only hurt nature, we cut ourselves off from nature. If we don't experience nature, we won't care about it. If shopping is the most popular out-of-home weekday activity, as Juliet Schor tells us, it means we're spending a lot of time indoors. Environmental writer James Swan says that one study found that Americans are indoors about 84 percent of the time. When they go to a national park, people spend most of their time in the visitor center and restaurants.

Shopping Takes Your Money

This one is obvious—shopping takes your money. And it is taking an awful lot of your money. Americans are in debt as never before and many have lost their jobs or are worried about losing them. The typical American household carries $8,500 of personal debt—excluding the mortgage. More and more people are filing for personal bankruptcy. More than 70 percent of Americans carry some sort of credit-card debt—an average of $1,700 per month.

Shopping Takes Your Time

Juliet Schor estimates that the average time spent shopping per week is six hours. But that seems low. Think of the people who shop for entertainment or because they're bored. In my workshops, people are shocked when I read this quote to them from Schor's *The Overworked American*: "We live in what may be the most consumer-oriented society in history. Americans spend three to four times as many hours a year shopping as their counterparts in Western European countries. Once a purely utilitarian chore, shopping has been elevated to the status of a national passion."

Since I have been cutting back on my shopping, I can't believe how much more time I have. And I never really shopped that much! I was a student most of my life, and when you're a student you have neither the time nor the money to shop. (That might be the best way to reduce our national consumerism—send everyone back to school!) Of course, it isn't just buying the product that takes time, but putting it together, using it, and maintaining it. When our daughter's VCR broke down, we gave her ours. My idea was to get one of those VCR Plus things, the ones that are supposed to be so simple to use. Supposedly, you just enter the numerical code that you find in the TV schedule and that's it. Well, the documentation for the product was about an inch thick. My husband finally figured out how to do it, but I never have.

We used to recoil at stories of how the Russians spent so

much time in lines shopping. However, when the Russians came to this country, shopping took them just as long because there are so many choices to make! I'm sure it was overwhelming for them to have to choose among 25,000 supermarket items including 200 brands of cereal. In 1990, 12,055 new products were introduced to American drugstores and supermarkets alone, a rate of thirty-three per day.

Shopping Saps Your Energy

Of course, time and energy are directly related. But there is time spent that fulfills you and time spent that drains you. And shopping certainly drains me. As life has speeded up, the shopping malls seem to get more confusing and overwhelming. Japanese people discuss the concept of *karoshi*, death from overwork. I wonder if there is a word that means death from over shopping.

A few years ago I finally had enough, and decided that I would just never go to malls anymore. But when I neared fifty, I realized that it was time to start buying my own underwear. My mother had always bought it for me, and I figured it was time for me to change.

It's hard to find underwear you like, and so I wanted to make sure I got the same kind she had always bought. I knew she got them at Penney's and there was a mall with a Penney's close to where I worked, so I decided to drop in one evening.

Do you know what happens when you haven't been to a department store for a while? It gets remodeled. Not to make it easier to find things, but to trap you. The straight aisles are converted into mazes, mirrors are placed everywhere you look, merchandise blocks your path everywhere you turn. I felt like I would have an anxiety attack. A little voice came into my head that said, "Run away, run away!" So I did.

I did come back later, but I went in another door closer to where I remembered the lingerie department was. Luckily they hadn't moved it. When I found the brand I wanted, I bought every single thing they had in my size. I didn't want to have to go through that experience again.

Who ever feels relaxed after a trip to the mall? You've been waiting in lines, the person ahead of you can't find their wallet, and it's a drag trying things on. The traffic and parking are always horrendous. In fact, the only time I've ever had an accident was in a big parking lot. A little car pulled out of a space too fast and totaled my car.

And then, when you get your purchase home, there's often something wrong with it. I got a hot-water bottle once that started leaking a few weeks after I got it. Do you think I ever found time to take it back? My daughter got a screen door and the salesperson promised her that all she needed to install it was a screwdriver. When she gets all set to put it up, she discovers she needs a drill! It's written right there in the instructions! Didn't the guy who sold it to her know that? Why didn't he tell her? I've concluded that stores just count on consumers being so overwhelmed with life that they won't get around to returning something that doesn't work. They think that we'll forget about it and end up buying another one.

So strike back. Do without. Shop less.

Shopping Reduces Ingenuity

It's challenging to find ways to "make do" instead of just going out and buying something. It is called ingenuity—being creative with the practical decisions that we must face every day. There is a certain satisfaction in figuring out how to avoid spending money. The person who whips dinner up from what's available in the cupboard is being creative. People who reuse envelopes, who create stationery from old calendars, who grow vegetables organically and figure out creative ways to deal with garden slugs—all are using their ingenuity. It's all kinds of things—the woman who is remodeling her house and goes to other sites to scrounge materials, the kids who buy a canoe together and then figure out an equitable way to share it. All of this is creativity.

We lose this creativity when we just run out and buy something. Who knows what that does to our ability to amuse ourselves, to operate in emergencies, to cope with the unexpected.

Shopping Produces Narcissism

When they shop, most people are shopping for themselves. Even at Christmas, it seems like half the purchases I make are for myself. For women especially, narcissism is encouraged because so much of our time is spent shopping for clothes. You're always looking at yourself in the mirror. It's so different from the way the majority of people throughout history have lived. We're always around a mirror, always seeing our reflection *all* of the time, and if not our reflection, we see the images of people in commercials that we compare ourselves to. There is a constant message to be concerned with your image.

Just think what that means in terms of mental energy that could be spent on something more creative. Just imagine what you could be doing instead of always wondering if your hair looks okay, what people think of your earrings, or if your lipstick has worn off.

Shopping Cuts You Off from People

The more you shop, the less you do other things. If you weren't shopping, you could be reading, gardening, working with the homeless, or taking a class. In particular, you could be spending time with friends. Shopping and television have just about killed our community life.

When you shop, you're usually by yourself. When I was in high school it was fun to go with my friends and try on hats and wigs. And maybe there are still friends who shop together. Usually, though, you're in a hurry and don't have time to just stroll around. And then, after a shopping trip, when you're back at the office or home, your purchases dominate the conversation. Instead of talking about real things in your life, you talk about what you have bought. It takes the place of a chance for real intimacy.

Maybe the most pernicious impact of shopping is that everybody has their own things. They don't need to share with other people. Consumerism has had a big boost from all the people who live alone in our country. Everyone has their own refrigerator and oven and car and on and on.

One woman told me that the happiest time in her life had been during the Depression, because everyone shared everything and helped each other out. That doesn't happen much anymore, and I worry that we have even lost our ability to share with others. Would we always be making such a big fuss about cutting taxes if we were in the habit of sharing with others?

Shopping Displaces Simple Pleasures

Just as shopping cuts you off from other people, it cuts you off from simple pleasures. Instead of singing, you buy a CD. Instead of making your own clothes, you buy what everyone else is wearing. Instead of growing your own fresh organic vegetables, you eat fruit imported from other countries where we send our pesticides. Once when I was asking a group what some of their simple pleasures were, one man described returning home from work and going straight to the garden and picking a ripe tomato and eating it right there. That for him was a simple pleasure that made life seem worthwhile.

Shopping Lowers Self-Esteem

Ultimately, consumerism lowers your self-esteem. Self-esteem comes only from developing your authentic self, and consumerism never encourages that. You're not taking the time to develop your talents, to be with people who care about you, to spend time on your spiritual life—activities that would boost your sense of self-worth.

Shopping Harms Your Health

Ironically, most Americans and Europeans suffer from diseases of affluence, with our lifestyle producing increases in cancer and heart disease. A report by the World Health Organization found that while infectious and parasitic diseases are the leading cause of mortality on the planet, heart disease, stroke, and cancer now kill almost as many people.

Shopping Undermines Commitment

Shopping cuts you off from the old and encourages lack of commitment.

Consumerism is always trying to get you to buy something new. The credo is that new is always better. Until concerned citizens got laws passed for historic preservation, we tore down anything in our way. We have so many choices, so many new brands each year. Does this mean that we don't commit to things because we think that something better might come along? Maybe because we believe that new is better, we've become dilettantes, never settling down to something. A new project is exciting; it's boring to try to complete the old project.

Does our fascination with the new even extend to our relationships with people? Does this orientation affect our divorce rate? Do we, even when we marry, keep looking for something better to come along? We can return our original product and get something new. We can trade our old car in for a new model. Out with the old, in with the new.

Shopping Makes You Unhappy

It should be clear that extreme consumerism just doesn't make us happy. It is reason enough to curtail shopping because it destroys the earth, but to discover that it doesn't even make us happy, that it separates us from the things that make us happy!

The underlying idea of consumerism is the idea that more is always better. If more is always better, that means you will never have enough, so you will never be satisfied. You'll never really enjoy what you have. You will be bored and cynical. You will always be yearning for something you don't have. When you have too much, you become satiated. No bike is ever as exciting as the first bike. Thirty sweaters a year don't get you as excited as just one a year does. You rarely have a sense of gratitude for what you have when you are caught in consumerism.

Understanding why we need to reduce our consumerism isn't enough, though. We also need to understand why we consume. What drives us to do it?

WHY DO WE CONSUME?

Think of the last time you went shopping. Not just to get something you needed, but when you went just to browse, to walk around. Think about why you went, what you felt like. I know I've gone shopping when I've felt bored and anxious. We're anesthetized by the ersatz music, the artificial lights, the bright unnatural colors, the white noise, the carefully controlled temperature. Thank God, no real life intrudes. We can escape. And it's so clean and neat, and the sales people are so nice. Why do I have to go home to that messy kitchen and those whining kids?

Not surprisingly, many of the reasons that we shop are similar to the reasons for not shopping. They are the other side of the coin. While consumerism decreases self-esteem, we turn to it hoping to *increase* our self-esteem. This is why author Philip Slater talks about *wealth addiction*. Just as in drug addiction, we keep going back to the thing that we know will eventually kill us. We get a high from it, but sooner or later the high wears off, and we need a stronger fix. I think of it as the Costco high! It's a cold and rainy Sunday afternoon, you haven't seen the sun in months, you're sick of your dirty house, so you go to Costco. It's exciting getting all that stuff for so cheap. But the thrill wears off, and next Sunday you're back for more.

Slater has said that we consume because we are empty and trying to fill up that emptiness. What is the cause of this emptiness? Much of our emptiness comes from not meeting our real needs for self-esteem and community. We need to feel accepted and acceptable, to feel that we have value, that we are unique, that people care for us. We all must have a sense of our own worth, a sense of being valued. But our uncaring society has undermined it. Consumption tries to fill this need in several ways.

Treatment in Stores

First, when we shop we are usually treated well in an otherwise inhospitable society. (That is if you are white and middle class. Poor people or people of color receive different treatment.) When we live in a city, we experience most people as rude or threatening. We shout obscenities to people in traffic, we push our way through the crowds, and, as night falls, we fear the violence and carry guns. Interactions with other people are frustrating and unfulfilling.

Symbols of Success

In our society, we think the route to self-esteem is to be esteemed by others. So when we buy lots of clothes, a big house, and an expensive car, we look like winners. The things we consume are like badges saying we are successful. They are the sign that we have *made it*.

Loneliness

Some people say they shop because they are lonely. At least in a shopping mall they can be around other people. So increasingly we see events happening at shopping malls—community colleges have classes there, seniors take their walks there, festivals are held there. All to lure people to this ersatz community.

Ultimately, community in a larger sense is destroyed because our materialism creates envy and jealousy. On one hand, it can cause violence—teenagers killing each other for a pair of sneakers. On the other hand, it makes people feel inferior to the person who dresses beautifully or has a nice car. Our consumerism has allowed some to get very rich and caused others to be poor, and there is community only among equals.

And so, with the increasing violence and fragmentation of society, we go to shopping malls where at least we feel safe and we're with other people, but we come away still feeling alone: the vicious circle again.

Estrangement from Nature

As we have moved into cities to be around jobs (as agribusiness has bought up family farms), we are increasingly cut off from nature. Places to hike and camp are usually miles away from where we live. And so people go shopping for nature, to try to fill their hunger for it. They buy camping equipment, recreational vehicles, bathing suits. It's a fraudulent experience of nature, but it's an attempt to fill a growing emptiness.

Maybe one of the reasons that we're drawn to the bright lights and colors of the mall is because our senses are starved from having no contact with real lights in nature.

Loss of Creativity

Since we have not learned to be creative in our schools, we feel we're being creative when we do something like remodel our house. But again, consumption is a substitute for really creating a place to live, because we usually just end up with a room that looks like a picture in a magazine.

So we shop because we are bored: we have little that really

excites us in our lives, that stirs us. We're seeking stimulation, and buying something is a quick form of it. We go for convenience and comfort instead of creativity.

The Convenience of Consumption

We shop because it's so convenient. Even though we might like to shop less, the way things are structured in this country, the alternative is difficult. Things are stacked against us.

While it is inconvenient to vote, we are making it easier and easier to shop. Stores are open longer than they used to be, with many open twenty-four hours a day, seven days a week. You can shop from catalogues using your charge card or fax machine, or click on the shopping channel, or shop on the Internet.

Our long workdays make it difficult to do anything else. About the only thing we have energy for after long days of work is shopping or watching television.

Our work has become so stressful and unpleasant that we are looking for immediate gratification to make up for the tedium of the day and poor treatment at work. It's just easier to escape to the mall than it is to get involved with a group trying to solve some of our problems.

The Force of Advertising

Finally, we shop because we are bombarded with advertising. In an earlier chapter, we saw the power of advertising. All the reasons I have just listed contribute to our vulnerability to advertising. Because there is so little sense of a solid self, we have become empty shells, open to the persuasion of advertising that tells us that if we buy we'll be happy. We have been duped.

Allen Kanner and Mary Gomes, in Theodore Roszak's *Ecopsychology,* compare advertising to Goebbels's theory of "the big lie"—if you repeat any falsehood enough, people will believe it.

Project the image of the totally happy consumer in countless ways and people will come to identify with it.

BECOMING CLEAR: REDUCING CONSUMERISM

And so, as we begin to try to live more joyfully and fully, we must first look at consumerism, for our extreme consumption is both a cause and a symptom of our diminished lives. Once we see this clearly, we are able to begin our search to find a way of life that will revitalize us.

How do we transform our shopping habits? It's not enough to just create a list of things you are going to do without. To begin to reduce our consumption, we must begin to fulfill our true needs— the need to live an authentic life, to discover our passion, to have community, to live in harmony with nature, to discover our spirituality. We will explore these in the next section, but first let's take a look at some of the ways people resist consumerism.

Avoid Advertising

Try not to expose yourself to the pressure of advertising. Don't watch commercials on television. Probably no one will find this an onerous chore. Even the most avid TV watchers must get furious about the number of commercials. A thirty-minute sitcom contains eight minutes of advertising. A two-hour movie becomes three hours on TV. Even if you tape your show and edit out the commercials, the message often comes through the program. A *Seinfeld* show can be built around Junior Mints, and a Klein bicycle hangs on the wall. As major corporations increasingly buy up television companies, they control what goes on in the programs.

Don't Shop as Entertainment

Beware. Even if you just want to walk around to pass the time, you won't get away without buying something. Remember, these people are experts. They know what they are doing. So never go to a mall just to pass the time. If you must go, take a list and keep your head down.

Research Every Purchase

When you research your purchases, you not only get some good information, it slows you down. You give that *lust-to-buy* time to wear off.

Develop Your Own Personal Slow-Down Mechanisms

One man put an X on the calendar a week away for something he wanted to buy. But he didn't label it—just an X. Then, the next week when he saw the X, if he could remember what it was for, he could figure out if he still wanted to buy the item. Some people buy only at stores that take returns, then they leave on the price tags when they get their purchases home. They just let their purchases sit there for a week, and often end up taking them back. One man enjoyed going through the store and filling up his basket and then just leaving the basket there. He would always feel so good about not buying all that stuff.

Take a List

When you do go shopping, take a list! Remember, one of advertisers' biggest weapons is our tendency to buy on impulse. How many times have you stopped by the store for a loaf of bread and a quart of milk and ended up spending fifty dollars? Take a list of questions along with you to consider before you buy. Make the list long enough and the impulse to spend may have passed by the time you finish it.

The Alternative Shopping List: Becoming a Caring Consumer

1. Do I really need this? Is there anything I can use instead?

Here's where the joys of ingenuity come in. It's fun to find substitutes. For instance, do you really need a nightgown or pajamas when a big shirt will do as well?

2. How will this item affect the quality of my life?

Will it help me engage in life more fully, like sheet music or gardening supplies or a swimming suit? Or will it just make me more passive—like an extra TV?

3. Is the cost of the item worth the amount of time it takes to earn the money to buy it?

This is the question suggested by Dominguez and Robin in *Your Money or Your Life*. For instance, how many hours do you have to work to buy your daily espressos? Is it worth it? You may say yes, but at least you've thought about it.

4. Could you buy it used? Borrow it? Rent it? Share the purchase with someone else?

Buying a used car can save thousands of dollars. Or, think of buying a car with someone else and sharing it. Or try to get along without a car and rent one when you need it.

5. Where should you buy it?

Consider these possibilities:

- A small, locally owned business that keeps your money circulating in the community

- A business you value, one that adds life to the community—like an independent book store

- A business that contributes to the community, perhaps by donating to a charity

- A business that treats its employees well

- A cooperative or worker-owned business, particularly one where you can be a member and have input

6. How will this purchase affect the environment?

- Is it biodegradable? (Compare your dish-washing soaps and cleaning agents.)

- Can it be recycled or repaired? (Don't use disposables like disposable batteries or cameras.)

- Will it use up resources to maintain? (A hand mower uses up much fewer resources than does an electric or gas powered one.)

- Is it over-packaged? Packaging pollutes, uses up resources, and swells our landfills. (If you can't avoid it, try leaving the packaging with the store.)

- Can you buy it in bulk and avoid packaging altogether?

- How far do you have to drive to buy it?

- Is it worth wasting your time and your gas to drive a long distance to save a few cents?

- Where is it made? How much energy was used to import it? Think of the energy costs to ship that pineapple from Hawaii. Do you really need a pineapple? When you do purchase something not made here, try to buy things made in Scandinavia, where the regulations on environmental damage are stronger than ours.

7. How were the people who made it treated?

Were they paid poorly? Was their health put at risk with pesticides? Were American jobs lost so corporations could make bigger profits?

Remind yourself that the more we consume cheap things from other countries, the less likely corporations are to make high-quality things in this country.

Some worry that if we reduce consumption, we're not being loyal Americans. But don't confuse being loyal to a corporation with being loyal to this country. We are forsaking our values of life, liberty, and justice for all *by consuming*, not by reducing our consuming.

If we reduce consuming, our corporations will have to change. They should reduce the wages to their top CEOs before we start worrying about their well-being. In 1995, many CEOs' income packages doubled as they laid off masses of workers.

Instead of buying an item, spend money for services that keep people employed. Whenever I eat at a small, locally owned restaurant, I know I'm helping keep six or seven people employed.

USE COMMUNITY TO REDUCE CONSUMPTION

There are lots of ways to consume less. When you begin to get involved in it, it becomes a creative challenge—much more fulfilling than going to a mall. You can get a real feeling of achievement when you resist buying something.

But it doesn't just have to be something you do all by yourself. Sharing may be the most important thing of all. Sharing not only saves money and the environment, it builds community, caring, and trust. In fact, as we know, it is the lack of those very things that drives people to consumerism. Here is where we can step out of the vicious cycle.

For instance, when my husband and I went camping for the first time, instead of buying a lot of new equipment, we borrowed from our friends. It was great. Our experience became a community experience. We got a tent from one person, a mattress from another, eating utensils from yet another. And lots of advice from everyone. And of course, when we came back, everyone wanted to hear what happened.

DEVELOP GUERRILLA TACTICS

When I was a kid I would show off to my friends by going into the post office during the winter and pinning clothespins to someone's heavy coat. Sometimes, when the line was very long, I would attach several, making a sort of long tail. I was thinking about that the other day, and I started wondering how I could have fun like that again, but make it work for the environment. We need to start stirring things up, get people to pay attention. I suggest we start using some guerrilla tactics.

We need to find something that will capture people's imagination. It can be something small like carrying your own cup so that you never use paper Styrofoam cups when you get something to take out. People are bound to ask why you are carrying that cup, and then you can explain.

Or it can be something bigger. On May 4, 1996, thousands of demonstrators closed down Paris streets as they lay down in the roads to protest air pollution. Skaters, bicyclists, and pedestrians demonstrated in cities all over France, blaming automobiles for the smog. Paris has 2.5 million cars, and up to 350 Parisians die each year of pollution-caused heart and lung diseases.

Or, we could think up more outrageous things. In the spirit of my childhood clothespin adventures, we could make up some little stickers that say "You don't really need this, do you?" You could take them to a department store and surreptitiously wander around sticking them in obscure places, like the inside of a blouse where the woman would see it when she tried it on. You wouldn't be harming the property because the sticker would peel off easily. A group of you could go out together and have a party afterward. It might even be as much fun as when you tried on hats and wigs with your friends in high school.

There is a group in British Columbia, Canada, who call themselves the Raging Grannies. They dress up like little old women with hats and gloves and then they stand on street corners and sing protest songs about nuclear waste or the cutting of old-growth forests to old-fashioned tunes like "Clementine" or "There Is a Tavern in the Town."

The Media Foundation, publisher of *Adbusters* magazine, sponsors the annual "Buy Nothing Day" on the day after Thanksgiving, traditionally the biggest shopping day of the year.

I think it would be a good idea to have a "Reclaim the Sabbath" day, advocating that shops be closed on Sundays or Saturdays—maybe half of each. The nice thing about this idea is that it could unite people across a broad spectrum of politics, including the religious right.

We could study past movements and see what worked. For instance, when women were working to get the vote in England, suffragists attended an opera one evening when the king and queen were scheduled to attend. At the end of the first act, the suffragists, who had taken an opera box high above the main floor, threw down hundreds of leaflets demanding that women get the right to vote. The security broke down the door to their box and took them out, but not before they got the attention of all the high society people who had come to listen to the opera *Joan of Arc*.

We need to resist. All the little things are important, but we need someone who will come up with a big campaign that will capture the public the way Cesar Chavez did with the grape boycotts. As the media are increasingly bought up by major corporations it's harder and harder to get the word out via the press. We can hope that the Internet will live up to its promise to help people organize.

THE NEXT STEP

Now that we have cleared a space in our lives—now that we have a vision of clarity for the kind of life we are seeking, now that we have begun to remove the clutter both within and without, we can seek out a new path, one that will help us discover how to live more fully and be fully alive.

PART 3

TRAIL SEEKERS

FINDING OUR UNIQUE PATH

Each man's life represents a road toward himself.
—HERMAN HESSE

After we have cleared some space in our lives, we begin to explore our unique path. That path is the actualization of the unique self. On that trail to one's self, we must develop authenticity, passion, and meaning.

The development of the authentic personality is vital to experiencing life fully. Without an authentic self, there is no conduit to the energy of life. The inauthentic personality, like a circuit breaker, stops the flow of energy. To be fully authentic, we need to discover our passion.

One's passion is like a light bulb that is charged by electricity. It's the light of the individual personality glowing brightly. Living one's passion is the ultimate experience of feeling alive and connected to the universe.

Meaning brings completeness, the feeling that you know who you are, what you believe, how you want to live. It allows you to resist the manipulation and pressures of the desecrated life, the commercialized life.

7

THE AUTHENTIC LIFE

> To be nobody but yourself in a world doing its best to
> make you everybody else means to fight the hardest
> battle any human can ever fight and never stop
> fighting.
>
> —E. E. CUMMINGS

Eddie was flying high. He was the best in the company. His ads for
the tobacco company were tops. He knew how to sell cigarettes.
And it wasn't just the success at work: he'd married into high society, and even though he wasn't earning much in the beginning, his
wife had her nest egg. They had a beautiful house, a swimming pool,
a sports car. And one day when he was driving, a giant hand reached
down from the sky, grabbed the wheel, and turned Eddie into the
path of an oncoming truck.

So goes the plot of *The Arrangement,* a novel by Elia Kazan.
Eddie could no longer stand the phony life he was leading, so he got
out of it however he could. There's much more to the plot, of course.
Before the crash, he had left his wife for a woman people thought of
as a tramp. Then, threatened with the loss of everything—his
money, his job—he goes back to his wife, and tries: tries to be the
husband he had promised to be, tries to be the success he had
wanted to be. But all this pretending only leads to driving into a
truck and nearly dying.

What precipitates all this? He saw something in the other
woman that awakened something in him that he had buried:

> At first I couldn't figure out whether she was very
> intelligent or downright stupid, or whether it made any
> difference. Clearly she didn't have a formal education.
> And that stood out, because the joint was full of Vassar
> and Radcliffe. These other girls, you never knew what they

themselves finally thought about anything, even after
you'd hit them with a couple of doubles. I mean they gave
out with opinions, but whose were they?

    Gwen, I found out in time, never talked beyond her
own personal knowledge. She wasn't handing down the
dicta of Max Lerner or that fellow Podhoretz or Alfred
Kazin or *Time* magazine. She talked from her own
experience and from what she'd figured out herself.
Everything she said, she really knew something about.
She'd had it rubbed into her, or been bored to death by it,
or been hit on the head with it, or had it rammed up into
her—or she'd have nothing to say on the subject. She
spoke her own truth and that was all.

Eddie finally does break free from his "successful" life. He
walks away from his job, his fortune, his family, and marries Gwen,
lives in a small town, runs a liquor store, and writes.

Have I satisfied my ambition? What was it? I have trouble
remembering. I hope that's because I've satisfied it. I do
write every morning . . . I don't feel estranged here
anymore. It's my place . . .

    But I do worry sometimes. Is this what all that drama,
that great overthrow was for—this simple living and
working, this day to day confluence?

THE NEED TO BE AUTHENTIC

Confluence: a flowing together. The feeling of connection, of completeness, of no longer feeling estranged, of being oneself. Jewish
theologian Abraham Heschel said that "sin is the refusal of the
human to become who we are."

    Why is this so central to the life of voluntary simplicity?

    Without an authentic self, we are always in search of a prepack-
aged self, something readily supplied by Madison Avenue—a false

self that involves consumption of the world's resources. Without the authentic self, we cannot meet the real needs of connection, connecting with our self, with others, and with a wider universe.

A MOVEMENT FOR OUR AGE

We'll remember the twentieth century for many horrible, horrible things: wars, environmental destruction, holocausts. But there has also been another movement, a life-affirming movement, a movement toward authenticity.

The civil rights movement, the women's movement, the gay and lesbian movement, the movement of people with disabilities—all these were and are about human rights. But they are also about becoming an authentic self, about being able to say "This is who I am," about not having to lie or pretend or hide. The plight of gays and lesbians shows, I think, the powerful need that people have to be known for who they are. Here is a group of people who risk being outcasts—and maybe even risk their lives—to be able to live an authentic life, to be able to quit hiding and pretending.

Even more powerful is the example of Alcoholics Anonymous, one of the twentieth century's major movements of human growth. It has at its core the affirmation of authenticity—"I'm Bob, I'm an alcoholic." Addiction is increasingly being seen as a descriptor of our lives—addiction to work, to shopping, to sex, to food—so maybe our real healing lies in being authentic. We all need to be able to stand and say, "This is who I am."

SELF-WORTH AND PERSONAL AUTHENTICITY

We all want a sense of our own self-worth. It's essential. But we've been given the wrong directions about how to find it. We think that to get self-esteem we need approval. So we tailor our personalities—how we act, what we say—to what we think will please others. We watch their eyes, we watch for the look of boredom or disapproval, the look that says we're weird or inferior, and then we fashion what we are saying to how they are reacting.

But it never works. Even if others *seem* to approve of us, we don't really achieve a sense of worth because at some level we feel that if people knew what we were *really* like, they wouldn't approve. So we have to keep hiding the real self, feeling ashamed and hating ourselves. The only way to have the kind of self-acceptance we're looking for is to develop the authentic self—to say and express what we really feel, what we really think, and then to act in congruence with those feelings—to be who we are.

A lot of people say that the desire to be authentic is what motivated them to simplify their lives. A former lawyer had been captivated by the downtown corporate look—hair in control, not a wrinkle in the shirt—striding efficiently down the street. She thought this was what she wanted, but when she had it, she felt like an impostor. It wasn't her, and it wasn't worth it. Professionals feel that they are posing, that they are impostors, and it becomes too painful. They often say, "I had to quit, it just wasn't me."

I remember something that happened early in my career—it epitomizes what I'm talking about. One day I was having lunch with the woman who would later become president of the community college (one of those people without a hair out of place), and I was trying to make a good impression, trying to appear poised, confident, efficient, and intelligent. But then I noticed I had been dunking my French dip sandwich in my coffee! What was I doing? What kind of a simpleton would she think I was? But then I thought, What should I do? Pretend I hadn't been doing it? Hope that she hadn't noticed? Pretend that I liked the taste?

I knew that probably nothing would work, so I gave a fake little laugh, and said, "ha, ha, look what I've been doing." (Actually, that cemented our friendship. I realized that poised, well-groomed people like people like me because I make them look even better.)

That experience and my response stand out in my mind as the quintessential snapshot of modern corporate life—always trying to create the proper image and usually failing. As John O'Neil says in *The Paradox of Success*, "The essential part of the mystique of business success has been to present a corporate happy face and an image of solid strength to the public."

Maintaining the image of success is the act of denying who you are. In the corporate setting you must always play a role, pretend you are something you're not. God forbid you ever have any strong feelings at work. If you expressed them, you would scare everyone to death. Your clothes are not meant to express who you are, but to define your status. Don't look too much like a secretary, don't look too mannish. And you must always look as if you have no real life at all. No wrinkles in your clothes, no cat hair on your jacket. Every hair totally in place. The further up you move, the shorter your hair becomes. My theory of leadership finally devolved into a very simple one: those who rise to the top are those who can control their hair— it's not so much a question of vision, as it is of hairspray.

CRUSHING OUR SPIRIT

It's hard to develop the authentic self, because it was so often crushed when we were children. That cookie-cutter mold comes down hard and flattens the dough out. I remember a soul-crushing experience in the eighth grade. We had just won a big volleyball game. I had played a wonderful game and I was feeling good as I walked out of the gym. My physical education teacher must have seen that gleam of confidence in my eyes, because she called me over with a stern look. "Cecile," she said, "You've got to quit being so loud and noisy. You've got to learn to be more poised and ladylike!" I can remember standing there, stunned. My personality was unacceptable.

Now think what that means. It means to stop feeling and expressing yourself authentically. It means holding back, repressing yourself, never expressing strong feelings, hiding behind a facade.

I set out to achieve that ladylike look.

As luck would have it, my family moved at the end of that year.

I moved from a small-town to a big suburban high school north of Seattle. I thought to myself, now's the time. I can change my personality and no one will know that I've always been loud and noisy. I can create a new personality; I planned to be extremely poised and ladylike.

Of course I couldn't sustain it. At some crucial point, I would wave my arms and knock a glass from someone's hand or trip going down the stairs or drop my cafeteria tray.

We all have stories like that. We all have a point in our lives when we decided we needed to develop a disguise for our real selves. For men it was probably a time when they lost a race or didn't get picked for the team or got pushed around by someone bigger, or turned down for a date by a girl—and then they set out to be cool guys—no emotions, no feelings.

Of course the pressure to pretend, to conceal the true self, continues into adult life. Think through your day. How much of your day is spent with your head bobbing—nodding in agreement at what your boss says, smiling in approval at what your colleague thinks—and all the while you're thinking, "These guys are crazy."

BLANDNESS OF THE SUCCESSFUL

Does being successful mean being bland? I think it might. I first learned this in the sixties when I met the most authentic woman I had ever known, a young, poor black woman. She said exactly what she thought and felt. She didn't try to flatter or manipulate. Having a conversation with this young black woman who had dropped out of high school and probably didn't read much was fascinating and exhilarating. She saw the falseness of the authorities and experts in society, so she became her own authority. She trusted her own perceptions, she expressed her own opinions. And they certainly weren't always flattering to a middle-class white woman.

Maybe she would have been the same if she had been a highly placed government official, but I don't think so. The higher you get, the less you can speak the truth. The reason she could be so honest was because she was not in the race for success; she was not shaping herself to be acceptable in the race to get ahead. In those days, trying to achieve would get her nowhere because there were no opportunities. So she might as well be herself. All she had was her integrity. I remember feeling that she had discovered one of life's secrets.

I was drawn to her because at the same age I had always had to hold back—not be too loud, too noisy, too forthright, too exuberant. My education had taught me to say only the things that were acceptable, that sounded intelligent; only to read the books that the English professors deemed worthy; never to espouse an opinion that wasn't approved of by a college professor. God forbid that you said that you liked reading James Michener or *Reader's Digest*. But this young woman was entirely herself. She had nothing to lose, so she said what she really thought. Thirty years later, I still remember her.

I've met that authenticity in men, too, and again it was not in "successful" men. The most authentic, open men I've ever met were men in Alcoholics Anonymous. Going to the birthday meeting—the celebration of a year's sobriety—of a friend I witnessed the honesty and authenticity of these men telling their stories. They knew that to stay sober they had to tell the truth about their lives. There was no pretending. With truth-telling came an acceptance of self that could never be found in the achievement of success.

Clearly, the more successful we become, the less we are ourselves, the more artificial we seem. Our clothes become a dress-for-success uniform, our opinions part of a party line. The more status we have to lose, the more difficult it is to reveal ourselves, to tell the truth. How much candor do you expect from a CEO or the president of the United States? What does it do to people to never tell the truth?

THE ARTIFICIAL ENVIRONMENT

After all, the whole force of urban-industrialism upon our tastes is to convince us that artificiality is not only

> inevitable, but better—perhaps finally to shut the real
> and the original out of awareness entirely.
> —THEODORE ROSZAK

Why is it so hard to be authentic? Why do we try to make ourselves into something we are not? It's not only because our culture of success discourages authenticity—there is something more. We are surrounded by an artificial environment.

Life has always been seen as a journey. What is the journey that we as Americans are making? Maybe our lives are like the stereotyped trips Americans take to Europe. Ten days in an air-conditioned bus. If it's Tuesday it must be Belgium. God forbid that our bathroom be down the hall. If we're lucky the shopkeepers will speak English. Maybe we can find a McDonald's for lunch.

We may as well be in Iowa as in France.

That stereotyped journey is very different from the journey I took to Europe after I graduated from college. Then I participated in international *work camps*—groups of students living and working together, providing a service to a community. One work camp was in Bordeaux, France. During the day we cleaned and painted old people's houses. At night the village people cooked for us and sang with us. On the weekend we went to the ocean and ate spit-roasted lamb on chunks of French bread and passed around bottles of wine. I was lonely sometimes, but the memories are so vivid. Hearing French songs brings back such intense feelings. I felt alive.

That was an authentic experience. The tour bus is not. How much of our lives resembles the tour bus, cut off from something real. We spend our lives in an artificial environment. The strip malls that all look alike, the canned laugh tracks that all sound alike. They're not real life. We are surrounded by a drab sameness.

The big slick hardware stores have replaced the funky old hardware store with junk piled high. These huge, efficient warehouses are not like the old store filled with lots of different and unique things like the one we have in our neighborhood—a store that was established after the Second World War. It has everything—hardware, shoes, dishes, sleeping bags, plants. Every year we buy our Christmas tree there for $4.99. The trees are all piled on top of each other and they are flat and funny looking, but it all seems so real and so fun. It's not a polished place—there's a comfortable shabbiness. But places like that are disappearing.

Our experiences are drained of all life and vitality when we are surrounded by such bland uniformity. McDonald's golden arches stand for American life more than the flag does. *Mc* is increasingly used as a prefix—until all we have is a *McLife*. Everything is slick. Since we are surrounded by tedious standardization, are we afraid to be authentic? How can we be real if we are surrounded by the artificial? Our inner selves are reflections of our outer reality.

Where are the people laughing and crying together over something real? We go to work in skyscrapers with artificial light where the windows won't open. Outside, skyscrapers block the sun. We drive home in cars, encased in steel, cut off from the outside temperature.

There is so much that is artificial in our lives: preservatives in our food, synthetics in our clothes, chemicals in our medicines. Maybe the American weight problem can be explained by the fact that we never feel nourished by anything, so we keep stuffing ourselves.

What does this artificiality, this flatness, do to us? Does it cause us to seek artificial ways to feel *something*? Does it drive us to violent movies and dangerous sex? Anything, so that we don't feel dead? Have we become the people we learned about in grade school—the Romans who cheered when the lions ate the Christians?

CUT OFF FROM OUR SENSES

When we're always watching television, we are cut off from real engagement with life because we are cut off from our senses. There are no smells when you watch TV. There is no wind in your face, no sun beating down. The goal of our technological society is to be able to control everything with a button, so we'll never be bothered by real life. Instead of getting out of our car and opening the garage, the click of the button opens the door. Instead of hanging out clothes, a click of the button starts the dryer.   ›

These seem like small things, but they drastically alter our experience of life. Many years ago, when my children were babies, I was up early one summer morning to hang out my diapers before it got too hot. I remember this experience so vividly. The morning was still cool, the sun was hot on my shoulders, there was a mist rising from the green hills. I felt so happy with nothing but the awareness of the hot sun and the cool morning air.

Ultimately we are cut off from nature: we have learned to see it as a nuisance, an inconvenience. Rain causes traffic accidents, a hot day makes us uncomfortable, mosquitoes are pests. We spend more time complaining about nature than we do enjoying it.

CUT OFF FROM OUR PAST

And something else that we don't usually think of: we are cut off from our past, a past that was much more in touch with real life than we are today. I realized this one day when someone came into my kitchen. I always felt a little apologetic when people first saw my kitchen. It's old, the wooden counters are scarred, the stove looks almost like an antique, but not so classy. A lot of my friends have remodeled kitchens, kitchens that look like a picture in *House Beautiful*. I'd never felt that I was trying to "keep up with the Joneses," but now I think maybe I really was. I always imagined that my friends felt critical, that they were wondering why I didn't do something about my kitchen. I felt like putting up a little sign that said, "I choose to live like this." A gesture that might have been a tiny bit defensive.

But as I was making some sort of feeble apology to a friend, he remarked, "This is what kitchens used to look like," and I thought, "Well, exactly!" I saw my kitchen with new eyes. In the past, kitchens looked like work centers. There was no worry about cutting boards with knife marks on them. Cutting boards were supposed to have knife marks on them. Your kitchen looked like you had done something real in it. Now, we want everything to look like a magazine ad. And of course to do that, we must spend a lot of money.

And what is *real* in the modern kitchen? We zap things in the microwave. We make instant brownies by adding water. Buying a steak wrapped in plastic, we don't connect it to a real cow. We don't even have to get our hands wet by washing dishes. We can stuff the dishes into a dishwasher and instead of standing there, maybe meditating, maybe listening to birds, or talking to someone, we switch on a machine and every other sound is drowned out.

ASSESSING TECHNOLOGY

With my concern for living authentically, it is easy to see why I've been called a neo-Luddite. The phrase "virtual reality" is awful to me. I want *real* reality.

So I have mixed feelings about technology. Theologian John Cobb, coauthor with Herman Daly of the book *For the Common Good,* says that high tech is basically in service of those who are devoted to profit and power. The ones who benefit the most are multinational corporations and the Defense Department. There is no way corporations could move our jobs out of the country so easily if they didn't have computers. There is no way marketing people could amass the data on us that they have without computers. There is no way money could be moved around the globe without computers. There is no way we could have fought the Persian Gulf War without computers.

The question that comes to my mind when I read about some new technological wonder is, Will it help me live my life more fully? Will it preserve and sustain the life of the planet and of people? Will it bring about more justice and equity?

Now, there may be good answers to these questions. The problem is, I don't really hear leaders in the high-tech field, people like Microsoft's Bill Gates, talking about them. He has referred to the Internet as a "shopper's heaven"! A shopper's heaven will only further endanger the welfare of people and the planet. Doesn't Bill Gates realize that our consumption is putting people into debt, using up the planet's resources, and polluting the environment? Surely he knows. Does he care?

We're obviously not going to get rid of technological advances. But we must begin to admit their ramifications, even in our personal lives. Essentially, technology makes it easy for us to live artificial, inauthentic lives. The Internet is lauded for being a place people can communicate freely, where no one will judge them for what they look like. No one can see if they are beautiful or not. But what do we really find? People assuming false identities trying to have virtual sex. A popular *New Yorker* cartoon shows a dog at a computer. The caption reads, "On the Internet, nobody knows you're a dog."

Some people have started Simplicity Study Circles on-line. To me, this cannot be. It's not a study circle if you can't laugh together, if you can't reach over and touch someone's arm, if you can't have coffee together and just while away the time. We all know that words are only part of communication. Emotions come to us in nonverbal cues we have all learned to read. We have to be face-to-face to read them. You can't laugh on-line.

Now, questions of technology cannot be answered here. But if we want to live fully, to live an authentic life, we must keep discussing them.

8

FINDING AND LIVING YOUR PASSION

Life is no brief candle to me. It is a sort of splendid
torch which I have got hold of for the moment, and I
want to make it burn as brightly as possible before
handing it on to future generations.
—GEORGE BERNARD SHAW

Most of us would like to end our lives feeling both that
we had a good time and that we left the world a little
better than we found it.
—PHILIP SLATER

The October 26, 1995, edition of the *Seattle Times* had a story about
a seventy-seven-year-old woman who discovered that she had acci-
dentally saved a million dollars. She did not realize she had reached
a million until her broker told her. How did she do it? Had she spent
her life pinching pennies, poring over the stock market reports, and
figuring out the best investments? Had she worked as a doctor or a
lawyer, earning big money?

No, for most of her life she had worked at modestly paying service jobs, and for the previous several years she had worked as a volunteer: at the age of seventy-seven she spent three weeks teaching
English to children in a remote Polish village. At seventy-six she was
part of the disaster-response team that went to Houston after a
major flood. At seventy-five, she learned cross-country skiing in
Finland. For years she volunteered as a *guardian ad litem* in the
court system, working for the interests of children.

She was simply more interested in life than in shopping and
spending money. And of course, hers is not an isolated story. More

and more people are realizing that high pay is meaningless if you don't get joy out of what you're doing. Read the daily paper and you'll read about the corporate vice president who resigns his job to teach high school, the college dean who resigns to live in the country and write, the executive vice-president of sales who turns her back on her $250,000 job to become a carpenter.

They all say that they've never been happier. And further, you will almost never find them at the malls. They simply have too many things that they would rather do. It's obvious, then, that the very best way to reduce your consumption is to get involved with your passion, doing something that you absolutely love to do, something that is much more exciting and challenging than shopping malls or television.

One of the core concepts of voluntary simplicity, then, is finding your passion.

Some live as artists traditionally have—finding a source of income that takes as little of their time and energy as possible and devoting the best of themselves to their passion. If they make money, great; if they don't, they keep on trying. As one artist said to me, "When the economy collapses, it's not going to make much difference to the artists. We're the cockroaches of society, and we can survive anything."

In fact, it was a conversation with a friend about artists that helped me decide to give up my well-paid, secure, full-time position. She said, "You should think of your teaching as your art. Artists have always been willing to sacrifice for their art."

And then, I realized, we should all think of ourselves as artists.

DOING WHAT YOU LOVE

Living your passion means finding something that you love to do, committing yourself to it, believing in it, and persevering, no matter what the financial rewards. It is something that is an authentic expression of who you really are. You get energy from it, you feel alive when you do it.

In *Uncommon Genius*, Denise Shekerjian tells the story of winners of the MacArthur prize, the so-called "genius" award. One theme runs through all their lives: the pleasure they receive from their work. They were unconcerned with money or fame. They would do their work whether they got paid or not. The book *Do What You Love, the Money Will Follow* by Marsha Sinetar, should have been called, "Do What You Love, and Maybe the Money Will Follow, or Maybe Not. Either Way, You'll Be Happy."

Quitting my administrative position has been wonderful. Nothing can compare to my days of reading, writing, and teaching. Even after several years, I still wake up in the morning thankful that I'm not heading off to the office to deal with the unpleasantness of politics, the malaise of low morale, the daily assaults on my sense of self. Cutting back on shopping and watching television just happened. It was easy to reduce my consumption when I had something so much more exciting to do—shopping is just an irritating interruption to spending my time working on my projects, and something I avoid as much as possible.

Voluntary simplicity is not what the son of a friend of mine assumed it to be: "What's that thing Cecile is involved in?" he asked. "That self-deprivation movement?" Voluntary simplicity is not a grim cutting back, it's discovering and filling the genuine human need to do work that you love.

DIFFERENT APPROACHES

Now, all people don't approach this in the same way. Some are looking for a *calling*, something they feel they were meant to do, something that is their *purpose* on earth. It's like a mission. But others don't particularly want an all-encompassing passion. Maybe they want two or three minor passions, something that adds spice to their lives. Others want "serial passions"—they want to throw themselves into something wholeheartedly for a while, and then move on to the next thing, feeling like they are exploring different parts of themselves.

The different patterns probably reflect one's temperament. I know that my temperament has always steered me toward an all-encompassing calling, and my passions have always been connected to teaching. Just out of college, I started out as an idealistic English teacher, feeling that if people read exciting books, their spirit would be awakened. Over the years I worked with civil rights, the women's movement, and now the voluntary simplicity movement, and I incorporated them all into my teaching. Of course, all of these issues are related—they all involve liberating people from the cultural dictates that keep them from living fully and joyfully. My passion just keeps getting wider and wider because each one includes the past ones. But there is one underlying thread: they have all been expressed in the learning opportunities that I create for people.

My husband has serial passions—music, computers, bicycles—and he writes about them all. My daughter always has several passions going at once, but her essential passion seems to be an ability to live life calmly and positively. Maybe enjoying life is her passion. My son is an artist and has never had to wonder what his passion is—he could be nothing other than an artist, so strong is the urge in him to paint and draw. Each one is being true to his or her nature.

But no matter what your particular approach, your passion is something that totally absorbs you. As Mihaly Csikszentmihalyi portrays it in his book *Flow*, it is something that seems to take you into another dimension. When you are absorbed in your passion, you lose all track of time, almost as if you were in a trance, and you emerge with a deep sense of peace and fulfillment. When you are absorbed in your passion, it's as if you are meditating. You forget yourself and your work seems to flow. You feel as if the ideas and creativity are coming from a source outside yourself.

Just as there is no one formula for voluntary simplicity, there is no one formula for living your passion. Discovering your passion is part of your lifelong quest for your authentic self. But there are certain things we all have in common. One is the barriers we face to finding our passion.

BARRIERS TO FINDING AND LIVING YOUR PASSION

Why don't more of us follow our passion? Why do so many people seem to be only half alive, settling for a life that is dull and boring? There seem to be two main barriers: one, people don't realize how important it is to have a passion, and two, people rarely receive encouragement to follow their passion. As a result, many have no idea what their passion might be.

WHY DEVELOP YOUR PASSION

First, people need to understand how important it is to develop their passion. Otherwise they are unlikely to persevere or take the risks they need to take.

If you don't develop your capacities, you'll be frustrated with life and you'll never feel excited and joyful. People who are pursuing their passions are the most happy, fulfilled people I know. The people who pursue only money or status never really are at peace with themselves. They are the people who never have enough. Once they reach one goal, they find it to be empty, and so they try to climb higher, earn more money. But they never get there.

If more people pursued their passion, we would have less crime, less dishonesty, less war, fewer hostile takeovers. The pursuit of power over others seems to come when you are not doing what you absolutely love to do, so you turn to substitutes for real gratification. In *The Paradox of Success*, O'Neil says that it is when people aren't really enjoying their work that they become ambitious and striving. Ambition is a spurious motivation masquerading as a passion. You can tell the difference by asking people if they would pursue their passion whether they were paid or not. If you love it, you'll find a way to do it no matter what.

Pursuing your passion makes you a kinder, more compassionate person. I realized this one day as I was teaching and found myself thinking that people in my classes always seemed to be some of the most fascinating, intelligent people I had ever met. As I was wondering why such an incredible group of people had found their way into my classes, I realized that it may have been more of a reflection on me than on them—they seemed special to me because I was enjoying what I was doing. And maybe *because* I was enjoying them so much, their true, delightful selves emerged, the true self that emerges only when someone pays attention and appreciates it.

When you are doing what you love, you feel more magnanimous, more kindly, less resentful and envious. When you are less resentful, you are more caring toward people. Think of that bitter person at work, the one who's doing the same old thing year after year, never taking any risks; the one who's always crabbing about other people, always finding fault, always being spiteful. That's the person who has never ventured to do what he or she loves.

When you feel more caring and positive about people, your personal relationships improve. When you're happier, you're just more pleasant to be with, and certainly more interesting. Your passion brings you in touch with kindred spirits, so your relationships are based on real interests you have in common—you have more to talk about than just the weather and the traffic.

And marriages, in particular, benefit because it's so easy for resentment to sour things—we almost always blame our spouses for anything that's going wrong. With so many people dissatisfied with their work, it's not surprising there are so many divorces.

When your life is falling apart, having a passion can keep you sane and whole. We all have hard times, when we're sick with anxiety or worry. Carl Jung said, "All the greatest and most important problems of life are fundamentally insoluble. Some higher or wider interest appeared on the patient's horizon, and through this broadening of his or her outlook the indissoluble problem lost its urgency. It was not solved logically in its own terms but faded when confronted with a new and stronger life urge."

Finding your passion builds community. My best friends are those I have worked with on shared passions. There's a feeling of closeness and community after the conference you planned is over, after the fund-raiser is over—sitting around laughing about the things that went wrong.

Living your passion helps your health, because positive emotions keep you healthier—not just the easier pleasures of going to a good movie or watching a ball game, but the deeper pleasures that come from being with people you care about, living your values, being creative, finding meaning in your life.

Expressing your passion gives you true self-confidence. Because when you are focused on what you love, not on your image, you feel confident. You lose your self-consciousness. Instead of being worried about the impression you are making, you're just interested in expressing your passion. We've all watched the violinist whose hair stuck out all over, but who couldn't care less because she was swept up in her playing.

Ultimately, pursuing your passion helps reduce consumption. When you have a passion, you're just not interested in wandering through the shopping mall. Your increased confidence helps you trust your own judgment and you more easily resist the manipulation of Madison Avenue. If you're involved in a painting or building a birdhouse, commercials can't touch you. The authentic self that emerges when you pursue your passion makes you more immune to messages urging a false image.

Finally, as traditional job and career paths continue to disappear, more and more people must find new ways to work—new, more creative ways to earn money. One trend is to have two or three sources of income. Maybe you have a part-time job that's not really exciting, but pays okay, and you know it's secure. Then you have a few things that you have developed yourself—maybe you make and sell jewelry and teach a class on jewelry making. As the rate of corporate layoffs continue to increase, people who have more than one source of income often feel *more* secure than those on a traditional career track, even though they might be making less money.

They're more secure because they know they don't have to rely totally on one income. If one source of income shrinks or dries up, they have somewhere else to turn. Often, these people don't go into as much debt, either—since their income varies, they are more careful of their spending.

Making money by this kind of freelancing isn't necessarily easy. It's hard to succeed at a small business venture unless you really, really love what you are doing. It takes so much commitment that you just can't fake the enthusiasm, so you'd better have passion for what you do. Succeeding on your own takes so much work, that unless you enjoy the work, you'll lose out or burn out.

So, as you can see, there are lots of reasons to pursue your passion. Unless people realize how important a passion is, they might feel that they are only being selfish when they do what they like.

This is what life is all about. As Brenda Ueland, author of *If You Want to Write*, once wrote, "Why should we all use our creative power . . . ? Because there is nothing that makes people so generous, joyful, lively, bold and compassionate, so indifferent to fighting and the accumulation of objects and money."

STEPS TO FINDING YOUR PASSION

There is a vitality, a life force, a quickening that is translated through you into action, and because there is only one you in all time, this expression is unique. And if you block it, it will never exist through any other medium and will be lost. The world will not have it. It is not your business to determine how good it is; nor how valuable it is; nor how it compares with other expressions. It is your business to keep it yours, clearly and directly, to keep the channel open. You do not even have to believe in yourself or your work. You have to keep open and aware of urges that motivate you. Keep the channel open.

—MARTHA GRAHAM, AS
TOLD TO CHOREOGRAPHER
AGNES DE MILLE IN Dance
to the Piper

One day, at the close of a workshop I was leading, a woman handed me this quote that she had copied down. Since then, I have seen this quote everywhere. Evidently it captures for us the direction we should be heading in pursuing our passion. Let's look closely at what Graham is saying.

Do What You Love

Dancer Martha Graham's words capture the spirit of the pursuit of passion. She talks about a "vitality, a life force, a quickening that is translated through you." Finding your passion means being irresistibly drawn to something, something that flows through you, catches you, and holds you. Your passion comes from doing the thing that quickens you, excites you, gives you energy.

Affirm the Uniqueness of the Individual

Martha Graham says: "there is only one you in all time." She believes in the uniqueness of each individual, something we must discover for ourselves. We don't decide on a personality and then create it. We don't check off the traits we want from a list. We uncover, *discover* our personality, allow it to unfold. I knew that former presidential candidate Ross Perot had rarely spent time with children because he talked about them as little lumps of clay, clay that can be molded. Anyone who has been around children knows that there is very little about them that is moldable. If we do succeed in molding children, creating them in the form we want, they become stunted and shrunken, as if they had been baked in the kiln too long. The best we can do in raising kids is to see them as flowers, to nurture the seed from which their full personality grows—if we have a daisy, we don't try to raise an orchid. We are all born with a unique self, and our path in life is to let it develop, not to block it.

Keep Clear of Competition, Reject Evaluations and Judgments

"It is not your business to determine how good it is; nor how valuable it is: nor how it compares with other expressions. It is your business to keep it yours, clearly and directly. . . . You do not even have to believe in yourself or your work." Comparing your expression to others, competing with others, doesn't work. We must try to break free of competition. We think we are encouraging artists by having competitions and judging and awards, but we are just putting pressure on them to play to the crowd, to measure themselves in terms of what others think. We are discouraging their unique voice.

In expressing one's unique self, we must not even think in terms of strengths and weaknesses. Career books talk of maximizing your strengths and minimizing your weaknesses. But what seems to be a weakness in one area is a strength in another area. To be emotional and creative makes a manager or administrator appear suspect, but these attributes are exactly what a teacher needs. Some people are neat and some messy. Some are calm, others excitable. Some like order, others prefer spontaneity. You must accept who you are.

It sounds strange to say, "You do not even have to believe in yourself or your work." What Graham means is that believing in it is irrelevant; the point is to love doing it, to be swept away by it. Believing in it has nothing to do with it. Martin Buber said, "There are no gifted or ungifted. There are only those who give and those who withhold."

Speak Up

"Keep the channel open." When Graham talks about creativity, she views it as something that emerges from being in touch with a source of flowing energy, something that you must work to keep flowing, something that could be easily blocked. One of the things that blocks this flowing of energy is failure to express yourself.

There can be no authenticity, no expression of one's passion unless we learn to speak up. You can't be who you are and just keep your mouth shut.

But who speaks up anymore? I ran across a quote by Virginia Woolf that made me yearn for some sort of good old days when people said things that had some substance and bite. Woolf writes to Lytton Strachey after reading the first six chapters of James Joyce's *Ulysses*: "Never have I read such tosh. . . . Of course, genius may blaze out on page 652, but I have my doubts."

But few will risk speaking up like that. The condition of the workplace has created such a situation of fear—everyone is afraid to lose their job so they are afraid to speak up. This has a horrible effect on the human personality. We come to despise ourselves. We lose our sense of self, and we block the flow of creativity.

We should all keep in mind the words of Sonya Kovalevsky, nineteenth-century mathematician: "Say what you know, do what you must, come what may."

Learn to Enjoy

"You have to keep open and aware of urges that motivate you." Graham talks about the "urges that motivate you." What does she mean? The most basic urge is for pleasure, for what pleases you. You cannot discover your passion if you have lost your ability to enjoy yourself. It begins as a baby with the pleasure of satisfying hunger pangs. The pleasure of being picked up and held. A child is not confused. It asks for what it wants. But then, socialization sets in. Love is withheld if the child doesn't act right, doesn't obey the parents, doesn't live up to the parents' expectations, and so we do what pleases our parents and we no longer please ourselves. As children, we are trying to figure out the world. We are absorbing a view of life, we are learning our culture. We want to know what is acceptable and not acceptable—so we will fit in, be accepted. Somehow we learn that we don't blow our nose on our hands or sing loudly in restaurants or spit at dinner parties. We absorb our culture.

And for most Americans, that means to compete and achieve, prove you are better than others, be number one. The thrill of winning is associated with the pleasure in our parents' eyes. Instead of doing what brings us *pleasure*, we begin to do what brings us *approval*. We start trying to achieve and win.

In our effort to be accepted and successful, almost everyone loses touch with what brings true enjoyment.

Many people don't know what gives them pleasure because it's been so long since they allowed themselves to experience pleasure. We have a strange relationship to pleasure in this country. Is it our Puritan heritage, the legacy of a culture that seemed to see pleasure as sinful? Are we unable to experience pleasure since we feel bad about having so much more than others? Does our low self-worth make us feel that we don't deserve to enjoy ourselves? Are we like slaves who lived under domination for so long that they forget what being free felt like? Have we so lost our sense of self that there is no self left to experience pleasure?

Or again, have we become so obsessed with maintaining our number-one position that we can focus only on achievement, on productivity, or getting ahead? Is this the Faustian bargain you make when you want power or status above all? Marilyn French, in *Beyond Power*, suggests that much of the power-seeking in our world—the behavior that results in corporate takeovers or wars—comes when people quit doing what brings them true enjoyment. Power becomes an artificial substitute for true pleasure.

To discover our particular passion, then, we must regain that ability to recognize what truly brings us joy. Pleasure is the key to discovering our particular passion. Start with simple pleasures. In *Healthy Pleasures*, Robert Ornstein and David Sobel show that simple pleasures improve your health, give you more energy, and improve your relationships with people. (In our culture, it's not enough that we simply enjoy ourselves, we have to know that it's good for us too.)

We must make time for simple pleasures: reading what you want, instead of what you feel you *should* read; eating what you want, instead of always eating what you feel you *should* eat; spending time with the people you like, instead of with people who will help you get ahead.

So start doing what you want to do. Do what you love the first thing in the morning—take time to start the day out quietly drinking your tea and reading the paper, watching the birds at your feeder. Make sure you have lunch with someone you like, take time to stop and talk to people at work, have what you want for dinner, go out to your singing group after dinner or attend a meeting of your bird-watching group, and never, never be without a novel to read when you fall asleep. When you begin with simple pleasures, you generate the energy and self-knowledge to risk the larger pleasures of creativity. Enjoyment is the path that leads to your passion.

Enjoy Whatever You're Doing

Pleasure, then, takes on a whole new meaning. Pleasure is the path to passion. But the inevitable comment is, we can't do what we want all of the time. Of *course* there are things we have to do that we don't want to do. But there's another way to think about pleasure. After you try to add more enjoyment to your life, what do you do with the big chunks of time left—the things you must do but that you don't particularly care for—like work? What if you've done all you can to get out of boring meetings, talk your way out of seemingly purposeless tasks? When you can't get out of something, then you figure out how to enjoy it. If you are working at a job you hate, you try to find a new job, but in the meantime figure out how you can enjoy the job you have—at least a little bit. Think of the people you have seen who have done that: the ferry worker who dances and twirls as she directs the cars, the cook who sings as he fries up the burgers, the bus driver who welcomes everyone on board.

Find pleasure wherever you can, because pleasure brings energy and hope and optimism, the factors you need to find and live your particular passion.

Engage in Self-Discovery

What you do need, though is to understand who you are, *because there is only one you in all time.* Unless you know your self, you won't know what kinds of things to do that will allow you to stay open.

In her classic book *A Life of One's Own,* Marion Milner, writing under the name Joanna Fields, sets out to determine what to do with her life. She realizes she must observe herself and reflect on what she finds. Each night she looks over her day and asks herself what she really enjoyed, what really gave her pleasure. Too often, she realized, she had been trying to enjoy something because it looked like others were enjoying it. Too often she saw herself trying to talk herself into things. Others seemed to like cocktail parties, so maybe she just wasn't trying hard enough. Other women seemed to like shopping, so maybe she wasn't feminine enough. Thus did Joanna Fields try to talk herself into things.

How many of us recognize this feeling? How many women have realized after a few years of marriage that they had talked themselves into marriage—not because they really loved the man, but because they wanted the status of marriage. How many men have discovered, after a few years of practicing law or medicine, that they had talked themselves into these careers—not because they really enjoyed them, but because they wanted the prestige of the professions.

And so, we are led back to the necessity of developing the authentic self. In the words of Herman Hesse, "Each man's life represents a road toward himself."

Take Action—Try Things Out

"Keep the channel open." The way to keep the channel open is to try things out. When I first thought of resigning from my administrative position, I didn't do it right away. I took a sabbatical of five months and tried out what it would be like to teach my classes and no longer be an administrator. So often we think something will be great, and when we do it, it isn't what we want at all. So try it out. Volunteer or develop an intern position. People say, "But what if I pick the wrong thing, or fail?" I hate to be trite, but I think that Miles Davis's comment, "Do not fear mistakes—there are none," is exactly right. Everything you do gives you more information. I think it's significant that a jazz musician would say that, because improvisation is their life. They don't know what they will be playing when the evening begins. They just jump in and play.

One way to start taking action is to sit with some friends and brainstorm some of the things you could do to pursue your passion. I encourage my students to think of something they love to do that someone would pay them ten dollars for. It's helpful to think in terms of ten dollars because too often when we consider something as a source of income, we think, "Oh, I could never support myself at that!" So we don't even try. But if we only had to earn ten dollars, we feel maybe we could handle that, so we go ahead and try.

One woman remembered my advice one night when she was sitting at her computer. She was interested in developing a career involving traveling, but she wasn't sure how. That night, there was a message on one of the electronic bulletin boards asking if anyone had any information about places to stay and things to do in Paris. This woman knew a lot about Paris, so she messaged back that she had a packet of materials available for ten dollars. Of course she didn't, but she got busy putting one together.

Persevere

But even though we have to keep trying things out, sooner or later we have to commit or we will remain scattered with our energy going in too many directions. Because we are constantly encouraged to indulge ourselves by shopping or watching TV, we don't always learn the habit of perseverance and commitment.

Everything written about creativity says that it's not the raw talent but the perseverance. So learn to block out those voices that make you doubt yourself. The voices that say, "Who do you think you are, trying to write? Who are you, taking yourself so seriously? You're no Van Gogh. Where's this going to lead? You're never going to make any money. Face the facts." The motto of the joyful and full-of-life actress, Ruth Gordon, star of *Harold and Maude,* was "Never, never face the facts."

Never ask yourself if you are good enough to do something. Only ask yourself if you enjoy doing it.

Stay Open and Learn from Life

"You have to keep open and aware of urges that motivate you." There is a certain Zen quality to finding your passion. It is sometimes out of your control and opportunities come that you must be ready to try. They may not be what you expected, but they may lead you places you didn't expect to go. It makes you think of Jung's idea of the collective unconscious, that when you are being true to yourself, you link up to other sources in the universe. When you commit to your authentic self, you discover your passion rather than construct it. Being authentic connects you to some wider energy in the universe and your passion emerges and, in Shaw's words, "life becomes a splendid torch."

9

FINDING MEANING

In a dark time, the eye begins to see.
—THEODORE ROETHKE

Why should we be in such desperate haste to succeed
and in such desperate enterprises? If a man does not
keep pace with his companions, perhaps it is because
he hears a different drummer. Let him step to the
music which he hears, however measured or far away.
—HENRY DAVID THOREAU

One afternoon, after finishing a particularly good lunch at a restaurant, I asked my husband, "What is your food philosophy?" He wasn't as fascinated with the question as I was. "What do you mean, food philosophy?" he asked. "What kind of a question is that?"

"Well, you need a food philosophy," I replied. "You need to know if you eat for pleasure, for health, for conviviality. How can you decide what to eat without a food philosophy? How will you know whether to eat meat or be a vegetarian, or what?" I could see he wasn't really listening, so I just continued the dialogue with myself.

I have always liked those questions. I like to ask my husband hypothetical questions like, "What would you do if someone offered you a million dollars to promote a product?" He always replies that no one is going to offer him that, so it's silly to even think about it.

Still, I think those questions are important. To find our unique path, we need to know our own values, but we rarely get a chance to think or talk about these kinds of questions. So we accept ready-made philosophies offered by television or religious fundamentalists. We need to be able to answer questions of meaning for ourselves: Who am I? What is my life philosophy? What is my purpose?

Answering these questions of meaning is central to living consciously and authentically. To deal with questions of meaning is to meet one of the fundamental human needs.

To live fully, then, we must search for meaning. But *meaning* is one of those words like *love*—it can *mean* so many things. There are at least three areas of meaning that we must deal with: gaining a sense of self-knowledge, developing a personal philosophy, and finding a sense of purpose. To develop our unique selves, we need to explore all three aspects of meaning.

SELF-KNOWLEDGE

Who am I? How do I want to live my life? What makes me happy? We need to understand our temperament, our likes and dislikes, our personality. Are we introverts or extroverts, do we like to read or go to big parties, do we need a lot of time alone, or do we like to hang around with other people? Without this self-knowledge, you have nothing to guide you in living day by day. There is no core.

This self-knowledge, this sense of who we are, must come from our life experiences. If we don't gain meaning and understanding from our own existence, we have a sense that our life is random and arbitrary, that we have no control over it. We feel anxious because we don't understand what is happening to us.

We're looking for the pattern revealed in our lives—the pattern that is unique to us. It is in our memories and past experiences that we discover patterns and find answers that give us a sense of direction. When we see patterns in our lives, we begin to understand who we are.

Often the answers can come from finding meaning in our suffering. Our suffering teaches us something about ourselves. Most of us gain our most valuable wisdom when we grasp the meaning that emerges from our suffering. A marriage crumbles, and even though we feel bad, we learn something about ourselves and are happier in our next relationship. We fail at a job and discover it wasn't really right for us, and find something better. We get depressed and go to therapy and gain insights about who we are, enabling us to live more happily.

DEVELOPING A PERSONAL PHILOSOPHY

Finding meaning is also about developing your personal philosophy, developing your ideas on what human nature is, what right and wrong are. Finding meaning is answering for yourself the basic life questions: What is truth? What is love? What is success? What is happiness? Without answers to these questions, you have no guidelines for living, and you will be easy prey for advertisers and other demagogues.

But how do you find the answers? You can go to the self-help section in the bookstore—it's overflowing with answers. But which one is right? How do you choose between competing ideas? The answers must emerge from your own experience.

When I worked in the South in the sixties, working in a poor, African-American neighborhood, I would visit the churches, and there I found my role models. It was those larger than life older black women with those strong, calm faces. They knew exactly what they thought and felt. There was no searching for words, no worrying about what to say. Their strength emanated from them and they acted without indecision or doubt. They knew what they thought and believed because their purpose was clear to them.

SENSE OF PURPOSE

Meaning is also finding a sense of purpose. It's answering the questions: How can I contribute to humanity, to the common good? How can I feel that my life makes a difference, that I will have left the world a better place when I die? How can I use my unique gifts to help others?

In college, like most students, I felt confused about what to do with my life. Then I read Viktor Frankl's *Man's Search for Meaning*, and it was a transforming experience for me. Frankl tells the story of how those who survived the death camps of World War II often had a higher motivating purpose that kept them going—they wanted to make a difference when they got out, to make sure the Holocaust never happened again. After he survived, Frankl developed "logotherapy," a therapeutic approach that helps people find meaning in their lives.

Finding a purpose, finding meaning in your life, is not only helpful to you, but to the community. Your particular source of meaning usually contributes to the common good. Sometimes the benefit to society is obvious—things like helping homeless people, for example. But it's not that simple. I remember reading a biography of Agatha Christie and thinking about her contributions. Had she contributed to society compared, for instance, to someone like Mother Theresa? At first I thought not. Then I remembered some of my sleepless nights when I was worried about something, and how I often got through the night reading a calming, soothing Agatha Christie novel. How can we compare her contribution to Mother Teresa's? We can't. They both contributed in their own way. So often, when you pursue your passion and find your source of meaning, you contribute to others in ways unknown to you.

MAKING A DIFFERENCE

The ultimate form of passion is acting on your values and taking a risk to make a difference. It doesn't mean just volunteering for a cause you feel is important because you think that you *should* do it. Involvement must give you increased energy and vitality.

Why don't we get involved, why don't we participate in this ultimate form of passion, making a difference? Because it isn't valued in this country, and because we don't know how to go about it. There is a program located in the Northwest that tries to change this. It's called the Giraffe Project. Its purpose is to encourage people to "stick their necks out for the common good." It finds people who have made a difference in their community and gives them publicity. The publicity allows others to see these people as role models and to become inspired and involved themselves.

Ultimately, we gain our sense of self-worth only when we act on our values. Voluntary simplicity calls upon us to think not only about our own lives and the life of the planet, but about others' lives, to be concerned with poverty and injustice. Committing ourselves to acting on our values is part of finding our passion. Ultimately we hope to find personal happiness, but it cannot be a matter of our personal welfare alone.

LIFE REFLECTION—THE CORE OF MEANING

The events in our lives happen in a sequence in time,
but in their significance to ourselves, they find their
own order . . . the continuous thread of revelation.
—EUDORA WELTY

It seems clear that to answer these questions of meaning, we need to engage in reflection on our lives, analyzing our experiences. Our schools have taught us to get our ideas from books. But books should only play the role of inspiration—inspiring us to learn about truth from our own experiences. We must learn to "read our fate," as Thoreau says, to read our life as if it were a book.

To really understand the concept of voluntary simplicity, we must examine our lives for messages about success. For instance, we may *intellectually* understand the problems of success, greed, and competition, but we don't fully grasp them until we have found the themes in our own lives. Then we understand the concepts with our whole selves and we can set out to change. Although the ideas about simplicity, authenticity, and passion may seem true to you, they don't really take hold until you find the need for them by studying your own past.

When I looked at my life, I discovered that whenever I pursued

our culture's definition of success, I ended up on the wrong path—
a path that did not lead to joy or peace of mind. But, when I tried to
express my authentic self, be true to myself, then I found that things
went well. I learned that Thoreau's words about the "different drummer" reflected my experience. I have learned that there is an inner
voice in me, an inner prompting that steers me away from a destructive path.

THE DIFFICULT GIFT AND THE UNCONSCIOUS URGE
TOWARD LIFE

Most of our lessons come from hard times. Sometimes when I'm
feeling very bad, a little voice comes to me reminding me that it's the
only way I'm going to learn, that I will be a much wiser person when
I emerge from the sadness and suffering. Of course, that little voice
makes me want to turn and shout, Leave me alone. I'd rather remain
shallow and superficial. I'm sick of wisdom. I just want to feel
better.

It's only later that we can look on times like these as a gift. At
the time, the experiences are too painful. We know we learn from
suffering! But who would choose to suffer? Yet, unless we learn
from these times, unless we find meaning in our suffering, the
suffering seems random and pointless and we become bitter and
cynical. Finding meaning in our suffering transforms it and transforms us.

The major turning point in my life came, as it does for so many,
from illness.

One day, I was standing in front of a classroom, teaching a class.
I had been sick for several weeks and had cut back my work to half-
time. I was very discouraged, and I didn't have much energy. But, as
I was standing there that day with my class, laughing and enjoying a
discussion we were having, I suddenly thought, This is the only time
that I feel happy. It became clear to me, in that difficult time, that I
was a teacher. That I needed to teach.

So I began to change my life. I had just finished my doctorate in education at Stanford, I was a full-time administrator in a community college, I was on several important boards, my husband had a prestigious job. I expected to move up in the hierarchy of the community college system. I was a success.

I thought I liked it. I thought I was happy.

But then I got sick, and I began to see things more clearly. I saw that I couldn't go on pursuing "success" because it didn't make me happy. In fact, it had made me sick. And so, I began to make changes. Ultimately, I resigned my full-time administrative position, and devoted myself to working with voluntary simplicity study circles.

Getting sick was the spark that began the change. It helped me begin to question how I was living.

But I had to reflect on that experience to understand my true direction. I could have ignored my experience and gone right on striving to move up the ladder. But by reflecting, by paying attention, I learned something about myself, my sense of purpose, and my life philosophy. I learned I was a teacher, that teaching made a difference in people's lives, that moving up the career ladder made me sick because I wasn't being true to my calling.

THE GENDER TRAP

Many of us learned to question society's mandates in our struggle with gender roles. Many of us learned some of our most important lessons about success from relationships between men and women. For me, it was my first marriage, indeed, the night of my wedding.

I had gone to have my hair done. (Hair again. Maybe our hair holds some previously unsuspected divination powers.) It was in the mid-sixties when they still sprayed your hair with lacquer so it stayed rigid on your head. When I got home, I started crying hysterically and brushed my hair out, destroying all the work of the beauty salon. Then I took my brush and threw it as hard as I could. I broke the ceiling light and the brush. I heard my sister ask my mother what was wrong with me. "Oh, she's just nervous," my mother said.

But that wasn't it. At some level, I knew I didn't really want to get married. But I didn't have the nerve to call off the wedding, which was only a few hours away. Besides, to be a successful woman, I had to get married. I couldn't risk being an old maid, being a failure. I was twenty-two.

The wedding went on as scheduled.

In the end, the marriage, which lasted for only seven years, taught me a lot about what it meant to be a woman in our society, and I learned, once again, to pay attention to my inner voice. It's clear to me now that the great welling up of feeling before the wedding was my true self trying to get me to look at the truth. Trying to get me to see how I really felt. But the voice of society was in my head. It was telling me, if you don't get married, you will have failed. Once again I learned that when I followed the acceptable path, I was going the wrong way.

BEING OPEN

But I didn't always have to be slapped in the face to pay attention. Sometimes I sought out new learning, pursued experiences that helped me find meaning, and was jolted awake and could see life with my own eyes. The message was always the same: the culture of striving and competing is empty.

One of my first awakenings was when I went to the South in the sixties to work for civil rights. As part of our training, we went to a meeting of the SCLC—the Southern Christian Leadership Conference, the organization founded by Martin Luther King, Jr. It was a conference about democracy, and I remember making an astonishing discovery. I realized that I had thought that I really understood the concept of democracy because I had studied it in college. I had studied the Bill of Rights; I had studied the Declaration of Independence.

I knew that the people I would meet at the conference had only attended school through third or fourth grade, so I assumed that I understood the problems much more than they did. I expected them to be interesting, but not very aware of the issues.

My smugness was shattered. The people at this conference had just come from the March on Selma. They had risked their lives for democracy. These people really knew about democracy, and book learning had nothing to do with it. I was the one who understood very little.

And then, as I continued to work in the South, I began to see the arrogance and lack of vitality in my own culture. I would go to a black church and hear people singing and see people dancing, and feel the joy and strength of the people. And then I would go to a white church, and I would think, These people must be sick. Their skin is pale, their voices are weak. And of course, these people who were upholding segregation *were* sick in a way, for their lives were blighted by racism and prejudice.

Prejudice is a part of a wider culture that judges people on the basis of their status—their education, their wealth, their race, their gender, their age, their sexual preference, their disabilities. Prejudice is a symptom of the sickness of the culture of success, a culture that does not value people. I began to understand that the more successful you seemed to become, the more vitality you lost. I saw that the successful middle-class white culture is often repressed and artificial. Somehow all of our life is drained out of us. We become bland and lifeless.

After my experience in the South, I began to understand something else. I felt isolated and alone. I envied the people living in this black ghetto. The civil rights movement had given them something. They had fought together for something they believed in. They had comforted each other in their losses. They had celebrated their victories together. They had something that I didn't have, and I wasn't sure what it was. They laughed together more than I did with my friends. Their conversation was about more than movies and restaurants.

Then I had another turning point. This time it was during the
women's movement. I was living in Cleveland with my first husband, who was attending graduate school. I had two little babies and
I didn't know anyone. I needed friends, so I started joining groups
for graduate student wives. The fact that I joined the gourmet cooking club shows how desperate I was, since I've never been able to
cook at all. After several dinner parties where no one even tasted my
creations, I looked elsewhere for friends.

I saw a notice in the local Unitarian church about a women's
consciousness-raising group. It was 1971, and people were talking
about a woman whose name we pronounced "Steinman" starting a
new magazine. I had read about feminism, and I thought it seemed
a little extreme. But since the gourmet group hadn't worked out, I
signed up.

Never before had I experienced such an awakening. I began to
understand how the cultural expectations for the successful
woman had drained my vitality. I realized I had gotten married
because I didn't want to be an old maid, the biggest failure of all for
my generation. And I learned not to blame myself. That there
wasn't something wrong with me for not liking my marriage. It was
not my fault, but the fault of the cultural expectations. I learned
that my values and beliefs about women had been constructed by
my society, and they were not in my best interests. Once again, I
learned that you had to question everything and develop your own
answers.

In that process of discovery, in that consciousness-raising
group, I once again began to realize that we had to struggle to break
free of the expectations and roles that society demanded from us.
Once again, I learned to question my culture's definition of success. Just as a fish is unaware it is swimming in water, I was
unaware of the tyranny of gender expectations. But when something runs counter to your true self, it makes you sick, it sours
something, and prompts you to question and search out a new
path.

CULTURAL SCRIPTS: BARRIERS TO MEANING

Society, and the family as its psychosocial agent, has to
solve a difficult problem: How to break a person's will
without his being aware of it? Yet by a complicated
process of indoctrination, rewards, punishments, and
fitting ideology, it solves this task by and large so well
that most people believe they are following their own
will and are unaware that their will itself is conditioned
and manipulated.

—ERICH FROMM

I had wanted to be successful. In the early sixties success for a
woman meant marriage. In the eighties, it meant a professional
career. In neither case, being married or being a professional, did I
find happiness.

I discovered that I had been living according to a cultural script,
a script that defined success in a very warped way. Our culture sets
us on a path, tells us what success is, and rewards us for conforming
to this script.

We learn the script well: be obedient, get good grades in school, go
to a good college, get a good job, make good money, have a big house
and expensive car. Then we will be successful and we'll be happy.

Most of us follow that script, thinking we're happy. People are
patting us on the back, so we must be happy. We're successful, so
we must be happy. But then something happens that wakes us up
and makes us see clearly that the script is wrong. We realize that we
don't like our job, our friends, our lives. Cracks start appearing. We
get chronic fatigue syndrome. We wake up at 3 A.M. and can't go
back to sleep. We have back problems. We have accidents while
we're driving. We have bad dreams. We feel angry a lot of the time.
We dread getting up in the morning. We get hysterical when someone cancels an appointment. We yell at the woman driving too
slowly in front of us. These are all messages from our true selves that
we are living by a script that is killing us.

In the end, I left them both—my first husband and my community college career. I had thought I wanted them because they were the route to being successful, but I discovered that they only made me unhappy.

DEVELOPING INNER AUTHORITY

I've learned to try to pay close attention to what I'm feeling and to trust that feeling, even if the voices of society are pulling me in another direction. When I decided to leave my marriage, when I decided to quit my administrative position, there were so many voices telling me to do the sensible thing. Don't change. Be safe. But that impulse toward health was there, and as the poet Theodore Roethke (whom I used to see hanging around the halls of my undergraduate English building on the University of Washington campus) said, "In a dark time, the eye begins to see."

We need to open our eyes to see clearly what is really true for us, the truths that emerge from looking closely at our own experience. From that we discover who we are, what we believe, and how we can make a difference.

And so, as we set out on our unique path, we must look at our own lives and begin to answer the basic life questions that have to do with meaning, that have to do with self-understanding, a life philosophy, and a sense of purpose. As we explore those issues, we begin to see once again that our American definition of success does not bring us joy.

PART 4

WOOD GATHERERS

When the stranger says: "What is the meaning of this city? Do you
huddle together because you love one another?" What will you
answer? "We all dwell together to make money from each
other," or, "This is a community"?

—T. S. ELIOT

I have perceiv'd that to be with those I like is
    enough,
To stop in company with the rest at evening is
    enough,
To be surrounded by beautiful, curious, breathing,
    laughing,
    flesh is enough,
To pass among them or touch any one, or rest my
    arm ever so
    lightly round his or her neck for a moment,
    what is this
    then?
I do not ask any more delight, I swim in it as in a sea.

—WALT WHITMAN

How can we transform ourselves from a group of people who "dwell
together to make money from each other" to a group of people who say to
each other, in Walt Whitman's words, "I have perceiv'd that to be with those
I like is enough . . . I do not ask any more delight, I swim in it as in a sea"?

We must learn to create community. We start as wood gatherers,
traveling on our unique path, but always coming back together to share
what we have gathered.

10

UNDERSTANDING COMMUNITY

> In the best communities everyone is a special person
> who sooner or later impinges on everyone else's
> consciousness. The effects of this constant attention
> make all, rich or poor, feel important, because the only
> way importance is perceived is by having other folks
> pay attention to you.
>
> —JOHN GAYLOR GATTO

Sitting on the porch on a summer night—the adults talking in low voices, the kids playing in the streets, the fireflies flitting around—it's one of the experiences I've never forgotten from my stay in the South in the mid-sixties. It was a poor black part of the city, so the houses were small and close together, set close to the street. With no air conditioning, people flocked to the porches. You could call to your neighbors and discuss the day, find out what was going on in their lives. Of course, you probably already knew—there were no secrets, since you could hear whatever happened in people's houses. If they were having trouble with their kids or with their marriage, you knew about it. And you could help out. You could keep an eye on the kids, and maybe the husband.

Most of us would be horrified to have so little privacy, yet I think of this when I've had friends tell me they are getting a divorce, and I've had no inkling. So private are we that our closest friends might barely know us.

In that poor neighborhood, people knew each other, they helped each other out, they laughed together, they held grudges, they forgave each other. There was true *soul* in that neighborhood—so different from the white, emotionally barren suburban section of town where I grew up. In that neighborhood in the South, we had street life, we had color. In my neighborhood the houses were set far back from the street, we escaped to patios in the back, there were no porches in the front. There was no life on the street. No sidewalks. Only cars. The only contact I had with my neighbors was when families united to file suit against a shopping center that was going to cut down all the trees on the adjoining land.

I did not even know what community was until my experience in the South, but that experience started me on a search for community. I remember walking around Chinatown in San Francisco, feeling envious because these people had community—the crowded streets, the jumbled stores, the people carrying their bags of groceries as they walked down the street to their apartments.

I felt envious when I read my Jewish novels because they had community. I loved their sense of history, the rituals, the shared traditions.

Then, in 1971, when I was looking for friends in Cleveland, I found the women's consciousness raising group. That was my great turning point. I experienced more community there than I ever had before. Here were people with whom I could really be myself. Here was a place that fired me up, made me laugh. I loved it. I got to know those women in a way that I've never known any one else. We could say anything to each other.

I remember one evening, three of us were out to dinner and we were talking about the sexual problems of one of the women. She was going to a psychiatrist because she had never experienced orgasm while making love. Well, we were sitting in this small restaurant talking about her psychiatrist's advice. He was recommending practicing with some sort of object of the "right" size. We laughed hysterically as we speculated about what would work, deciding candles would be best. And so economical too—they could be used later for dinner parties, even if they *were* slightly bent.

Well, we looked around and every one was silent. The whole restaurant was listening to our conversation. They were mesmerized. Now, I know it wasn't really *just* the subject matter that was catching their ear, I know that they were wishing that *they* could be having such an intimate, alive conversation themselves. Only when you experience community can you have that kind of conversation.

DEFINITION BY THE PEOPLE

Many people are talking about community, but by and large it is the sociologists and psychologists—the experts and authorities—who are defining it. But true change must grow out of people's experience. Let's look at the way simplicity circle members have defined community. Here's what they had to say when I asked them to describe a time in their life when they had experienced community. I didn't define community *for* them, their definitions grew from their own experience.

One woman's experience of community was on the bus—a bus commute involving a ferry connection, a commute that lasted over an hour. The bus driver knew everyone, chatted with everyone, asked after people's health if they missed a day. During the ferry ride, someone would get coffee for everyone and they would sit and talk.

For this woman community meant feeling a part of the group, seeing the real person; it was a commitment to each other, the experience of laughing together, being happy to see each other, and feeling valued. The positive thing about this kind of community is that it was with a group of people who had randomly come together. These people didn't share the same jobs or the same neighborhoods. By creating community, they made something special out of a common, ordinary occurrence. Creating community on that bus ride redeemed a potentially boring or wasted stretch of time.

One young man described a very different experience of community, but there was something he shared in common with the woman on the bus. It was "forced down-time." For him it came when there was no wind on the sailing ship he crewed. Although the community emerged in a number of ways—working together, having a common goal, sharing a sense of accomplishment, and laughing together—the real glue that bound them together was the fact that they couldn't escape each other. This is just what the bus commuters experienced—they couldn't escape, either. They simply were forced to spend time together, whether they wanted to or not, and oddly, this contributed to the experience of community rather than detracting from it.

It makes me think about how anxious we are in American society to always have an escape hatch, to get out of something if we don't like it. That's part of our national character, I guess—our country grew because people ran away from somewhere else. That gives us our adventurous character, but maybe it also means that we have a hard time building community because we escape if things get uncomfortable. I've seen concerts where people don't even sit down for the whole thing. They just get up and leave if things start dragging. I myself always sit on the edge of the crowd at lectures in order to escape if I get bored.

Yet here were people who found community *because* they couldn't escape each other.

One woman recalled her years growing up in a Quaker school where they had shared decision-making, worked by consensus, engaged in service to the community, and did physical work together. To her, community was defined by the consensus and shared decision-making, but she realized that these factors were greatly enhanced by doing physical work together, and indeed, this factor of working together was a theme that constantly emerged.

In fact, it may be the best way to learn the art of cooperation, because everyone *must* cooperate to finish a project. You can actually see the results of cooperation. Quakers have always sponsored programs that build community through working together, using as their slogan the poet Kahil Gibran's words "Work is love made visible." Where people have difficulty talking together, they can often form bonds by working together.

Sometimes community emerges when people band together to help just one person. An older woman recalled the support and commitment from her friends when they thought her newborn grandchild was going to die. Her friends told her that they would be there with her every day until the crisis was past. And they were.

We all know that feeling, at least somewhat—how a friend's tragedy pulls a group together. We've seen community grow as the gays fight AIDS. Some people have even expressed a nostalgia for their experiences in Vietnam. Life became precious as people faced death daily together.

One woman fondly recalled a religious commune she had joined when she was younger, a kind of a "hippies for Jesus" group. She was sad because she had never been able to re-create that community again. Nowhere else was she able to find the shared values, the caring for one another, and the sense of belonging that she had felt with that group.

Hearing stories such as these makes us better understand the appeal of the religious right in this country. Somehow, we must create that feeling of caring in developing, and it's something that people are finding in simplicity circles.

Several people recalled the intense community formed by survivors of earthquakes. They valued the caring and concern people had for each other—people risked their lives to save people, shared their food, shared their shelter, and once again—they told stories. People dropped their masks and became real to others.

There are so many stories of community that it gives you hope. If we can help people remember their experiences of community, of their experiences of living together in a college dorm, helping each other out in the snow (with everyone in their pajamas), or being in recovery programs, maybe we will be able to rebuild the experience of community in our current lives.

DEFINING COMMUNITY

So what is community? What can we learn from people's experiences? Community is many things, but the underlying theme is the feeling of being valued, of feeling accepted, of being cared for.

Real community involves equality, participation, authenticity and sharing—the sharing of values, of laughter, of problems, of food, of stories.

In community, people become equals. There is nothing like an earthquake or a high wind on a sailboat to strip away status differences.

In community, people's authenticity emerges. You can't pretend to be emotionally cool when you're fighting a forest fire or piling up sand bags to stop a flood.

Perhaps when we respond as a community to these natural disasters, it is nature teaching us something—that if we are going to survive we must build communities of caring and connection.

WHY HAVE COMMUNITY?

Can we begin to see why having community is important? It's important if for no other reason than our own personal survival. For instance, in the early 1960s researchers found that a small town in Pennsylvania, called Roseto, had a rate of heart disease much lower than the national average. It also seemed more resistant to ulcers and senility. After searching for the reason, researchers concluded that the magic ingredient was a sense of community. Other research has confirmed this. Doctors have found that support groups improve the health of people suffering from heart disease and that the lives of cancer patients are prolonged by support groups.

So the health benefits of community can be confirmed by

research. Other benefits are more subtle—benefits such as feelings of self-worth and dignity. But without community, we will all feel alone and insecure and continue to see life as a battleground in which we must continue working, competing, and accumulating things. We'll never quit consuming until we feel the security of community.

WHAT KEEPS US FROM COMMUNITY?

As I hear people in study circles talking about their experiences of community, I can hear their yearning. We would love to have more community. What are the forces stopping us? Once again, study-circle members had some interesting answers.

Cars

We know this is true, because any time you cut back on your driving, you experience more community. When you walk in your neighborhood, you see your neighbors. When you take the bus, you build community. I've started asking people to give me rides when we are both going to the same event. Do they mind? Most people not only like the company, they feel safer.

Television

We are simply not available for other people when we are watching TV. But I think there is something else. TV destroys community because it makes real life seem dull compared to TV. People feel closer to characters on TV because they know them better and their lives are simply more interesting than the lives of real people. Life on TV is more intense and exciting.

When we spend a lot of time with television, we lose our ability to carry on good conversation, and as a result, spending time with others becomes even less interesting—and even somewhat stressful. It's uncomfortable when you don't know how to talk together.

Television makes dropping in on your neighbor hard. First, you're afraid you might interrupt their favorite show, and second, TV creates artificially high housekeeping standards that none of us can meet. When I was a kid, our house wasn't neat, but my mother didn't mind people dropping in. The television image of the perfect house hadn't taken hold.

Technology

We're spending time with machines instead of people. Communication on the Internet may have some value, but it just cannot replace face to face time spent with real people.

Technology has created a world devoted to convenience and comfort. Every possible physical chore has been eliminated. We don't push our lawn mowers; we don't walk to the store and carry our groceries home; and we don't hang out our clothes. There's a machine that we hook up to do every one of those things. So technology has meant that we do less physical work—and as I found in my experience, doing physical work together builds community.

As we saw, community often grows from facing something dangerous or difficult together. Our modern comforts and conveniences have taken away the intensity of our lives, making our lives bland. When our lives are bland, our response is weak, we quit caring. As the author Storm Jameson said, "It is an illusion to think that more comfort means more happiness. Happiness comes of the capacity to feel deeply, to enjoy simply, to think freely, to be needed."

And it's not just computers, it's technological advances like air-conditioning. With air-conditioning, people have quit sitting outside on their porches, and we've even quit *building* porches. With garage openers people can disappear into their homes without having to say hello to their neighbors. As cars have become more high tech, you don't see as many boys and men hanging out fixing their car engines.

Finally, technology is destroying community in the workplace.

Not only is there little physical work to do together, not only are we spending more time at the computer screen, technology performs the dual function of robbing us of our work and pressuring us to work harder, giving us less time for others. When people are laid off because of technology, some retreat to the shame and loneliness of unemployment, and the ones left are buried beneath mountains of work. Neither builds community.

And of course, technology makes possible the multinational corporations that have destroyed local businesses and replaced them by giant, impersonal shopping complexes. You will never know the people who work at Wal-Mart the way people used to know the each other at the corner grocery store.

As technology has increased the speed and frenzy in our lives, we not only have less time for each other, we behave badly toward each other. Philip Slater makes the observation in his book *The Pursuit of Loneliness* that our lives are so crowded and frenetic that contact with other people becomes negative rather than positive. Insecurity at work brings out back-biting; competition in schools makes people enemies rather than friends; traffic jams find us shouting obscenities to other people; long lines makes us impatient and rude to others who we think are moving too slowly.

Our experience of others becomes so negative that we spend our private lives trying to escape from each other. As a result, we get lonelier and lonelier.

Ultimately, we can blame our affluence. When people are affluent, they just don't need each other as much. When you don't need each other, you don't share with each other. Affluence brings bigger houses built farther apart—in the last twenty years, new houses have doubled in size. Affluence even destroys community in the family, because everyone ends up having their own phone, their own TV. I knew some parents who didn't want to argue with their daughter about the TV, so she got her own TV. They didn't want to argue about the phone, so she got her own line. And of course, she needed the computer the most, so it went into her room. I used to think of her sitting all alone up in her room, surrounded by her machines. (Maybe her parents communicated with her by fax.) You're *supposed* to be arguing about the TV and the phone. That's what you do in families. The parents divorced after their daughter grew up.

Mobility

Our mobility undermines community. When people are constantly moving, we just don't get to know them as well. For instance, in our neighborhood, we have a strong feeling of community. But one day, a couple started talking about moving, and I immediately felt myself pull away from them. I realized that I was unwilling to put time into a relationship that might end.

No Places to Hang Out

People don't hang out in cafes much any more. We're just too busy. On the other hand, maybe we would hang out if there were more cafes around. We have a local cafe in our neighborhood that is filled from 6 A.M. till 11 P.M. The owners of the Honey Bear don't see themselves just in the business of selling food, they also see their role as creating community. They see themselves as one of the *great good places* that hardly exist anymore. Those of us who have quit our "real" jobs have our meetings at the Honey Bear, people meet friends at the Honey Bear, and people gather in the evening to hear music there. Everyone in town knows about the Honey Bear.

Why aren't there more cafes? More and more chains are making it difficult for the small, neighborhood business to survive. As the chains drive out local businesses, the stores and restaurants all start looking the same. Some franchises are setting up pseudo-cafes. But who wants to hang out in a franchise where there is no uniqueness or authenticity or soul?

TAKING CONTROL

There are many reasons, then, for the fact that we have so little community. But, if there is anything that we can take action on, it is forming community. It's hard to save the environment, it's hard to have meaningful work or find our passion, but we can all build community.

11

BUILDING COMMUNITY

A friend is not someone
Who is taken in by sham,
A friend is one who knows your faults,
And doesn't give a damn.

—ANONYMOUS

Like so many others, my husband and I wanted a greater sense of community in our lives. So we joined a book club. We managed to participate regularly for three years, but then we dropped out. We discovered we had begun to dread going. Instead of an informal, supportive, conversational setting, the group created a pseudo-college English class. Each meeting got worse—I began to feel like my grade was on the line, that if I said something others thought was stupid, I would get a C minus. But this wouldn't be just a grade. It would actually mean my friends would reject me. I dreaded sneers and sarcastic remarks. I worried they would think my book selection was stupid, let alone my comments about it. I felt that after three years we should have known each other better, but instead, I felt I knew the people in the club less.

So when my neighbors talked of starting a book club, I said no, no, no. We started a video club instead. On the last Friday night of each month, we gather together and watch a movie on video. Now, sometimes the pressure's on to select a video that everyone likes, but at least our friendship isn't on the line.

What we do in the video group that we had quit doing in the book club is laugh. That's the absolute basic requirement for me in community. If we're not laughing, I'm not going to do it.

Laughing means people are enjoying each other. It brings a state of felicity, of delight. You feel glad to be alive and you think, this is it! You just don't need much more than this—a group of friends enjoying each other.

But laughter is really an indicator of something more basic: of people accepting each other. You are valued because you are alive, not because of how much money you earn or how big your house is. When we have that sense of being valued, of being connected, we don't live lives of consumerism and ambition. We don't need to *prove* that we have worth.

I learned this many years ago when I was looking through my father's things. My father had died in an airplane crash when I was eight and left his trunk from the war years when he had been a pilot in World War II. One day, when I was rummaging through his trunk, I found a quote in a little picture frame: "A friend is not someone who is taken in by sham, a friend is one who knows your faults, and doesn't give a damn."

There it was, it seemed to me, the key to community. We must have a group of people to whom we can express our true selves. We must have a group of caring people who affirm our true selves.

Of course, neighbors are perfect for this. They know things about you that no one will ever know at work. They see your house in its real state. They see you in your ratty clothes. And you can really help each other out. You can help out in little ways, like taking care of someone's dog or buying their kid's school candy. Or you can help in bigger ways, like comforting them when a family member dies.

There will be different kinds of communities. There is potential for community at work, in your church, in your neighborhood, in your professional organizations. But none of these groups will develop into a community unless people learn the skills for building community. We can learn those skills by exploring the ways people are building community.

URBAN VILLAGES

There is a lot of new community growth in what I am calling urban villages. This is an area smaller than the public arena, and larger than a neighborhood. It might take in several neighborhoods and be a distinct part of town. In these areas people are organizing food co-ops, community gardens, tool banks, and systems of bartering.

In their book *The Quickening of America*, Frances Moore Lappe and Paul Dubois tell the stories of community councils organizing to protest city actions and to lobby for resources in their community. In many cities, neighborhood departments fund local community efforts, giving them money to clean up the neighborhood and paint and prune trees.

Strong neighborhood centers can bring alive this concept of an urban village. In my neighborhood there is a center that is located in a former elementary school, called the Phinney Neighborhood Association. It brings so much life to the wider neighborhood. This former school has been turned into a gathering place with lots of activities and classes. There's day care in the morning and a coffeehouse with music at night. Any evening you can find yoga in one classroom, salsa dancing in another, a string quartet in another, and simplicity circles in another. To get to the classes you walk through an ever-changing art show. On weekends there are flea markets and plant exchanges and mystery novel swaps. The center organizes work parties to fix up the homes of people with disabilities and to work with a local church to feed and house the homeless. There's a "well home" program with tool rentals and do-it-yourself classes. The center organizes dinner "circles" for people, sponsors a garden club, holds gallery walks, sponsors street cleanups, holds classes on bicycle maintenance, and sponsors community meetings on earthquake safety.

There is a paid staff, but the money to pay them has been generated by neighborhood involvement in the programs. Every urban village needs a physical place to gather and any community could do this.

NEIGHBORHOOD

All these levels of community are important, but maybe the easiest way we can begin to create community is at the neighborhood level or in our homes. This is something we can do by just walking across the street and inviting a couple of our neighbors over. It's hard, isn't it? You feel like you're interrupting or imposing or coming to beg for someone's company. There seems to be an embarrassment about needing to have friends. Is our individualism so extreme that we are ashamed of a basic human need? Or is it the fear of rejection that makes inviting friends over so hard? You worry that maybe they have something better to do than come to your house.

It's interesting to think about your own experiences of neighbor-hood. The most community-oriented place I ever lived was graduate-student housing. The apartment complexes were built around court-yards of grass with little playgrounds of slides and swings in the middle. Through the grass ran a curving sidewalk for the older kids to ride bikes while the little ones played in the sand in the center. We each had little fenced patios with picnic tables, and since we were in California, we ate outside a lot. Of course, you could often hear your neighbors through the walls, but that gave it kind of a cozy feeling. The smallness of the units made it even cozier. Since they were *all* small, there was no feeling of inadequacy or inferiority about someone having a bigger house than you. We got to know our neighbors really well.

I realized how much easier it was to develop community there than it was where I had lived growing up, out in the suburbs—big houses set back from the streets, double door garages opened by remote control, big lawns with patios in the back. There you could avoid ever having to meet a neighbor if you didn't want to, and of course if you *did* want to, it would be pretty hard to make contact. If you got lonely during the day and thought about popping into a store for a loaf of bread, there was no place you could walk to, and even your car only took you to huge shopping centers where you couldn't get to know anyone anyway.

What were we thinking about? Was this all planned by major retailers? Suburban living practically guaranteed that we would become a nation of shoppers. We had to buy lots of cars, first. Then, the one family–one house idea we aspired to meant we all bought our own appliances. In order to combat the loneliness of the streets, you spent more time at the shopping malls. It's depressing to even think about it.

Today city planners are coming up with some new ideas. For lots of places it's too late, but new developments could benefit. Sometimes old places can adapt a few of the ideas.

Streets

It's easier to call back and forth across the street when streets are narrow. Wide streets mean people can drive too fast, endangering the lives of kids and pets. In Seattle we have put in a lot of planter circles at intersections, forcing people to slow down and proceed carefully. Neighbors take charge of these areas and work together to keep flowers blooming and weeds pulled.

With smaller lots and narrower streets, we would have extra space for neighborhood parks. When my kids were little, I lived in Cleveland, and there seemed to be a pocket park on almost every corner—a few slides and swings and a sand box where you could sit and talk to other mothers while the kids played. Stay-at-home mothers just didn't get as depressed as they often do when there is no one to talk to.

Neighborhood Stores

For many years we've lived in a neighborhood that has a little grocery store. It's a part of a larger co-op system, so it has lots of organic foods and bulk items. You know all the checkers by name and sometimes they even help coordinate your shopping. It was not unusual for my husband to stop by the store right after I had been there. The checker would tell him, "Oh, Cecile already got that." Or if I was in the store when Paul came in, they would get on the loudspeaker and announce, "Cecile, Paul's here in the store."

And you can walk to a neighborhood store. When you walk, you not only get exercise, save on pollution and car expenses, you also get to visit with neighbors along the way. Having a neighborhood store certainly improves my social life. I don't think I've ever made a trip to that little store without running into a friend. I can have a great social life on Saturday night just hanging out by the produce.

Town Centers

One of the nicest places for me to walk is a neighborhood shopping district about two miles from my house. It's a place with interesting shops and cafes—there are restaurants, grocery stores, drug stores, used bookstores, a video rental store, and a library where the librarians call me by name. In fact, this area has the only shopping mall I've ever liked. They have taken an old school and put shops on the bottom and middle floors and apartments on the top. It's small enough so that you can get to know the shop owners. The bookstore even rents out books and so I can get new mysteries without having to wait. Close by is a tea shop with lots of tables where people can hang out and read at all hours.

Celebration

We must start bringing back fun things that build community— conversation, singing, dancing, storytelling, games. I have a friend— she's French, so maybe that's why she can get away with it—who has singing parties. First we sing a song in French and then one in English (after having great French food that everyone brings). When I told my other friends about the singing parties, and suggested that we have one too, I mainly got strange looks. They were worried, of course, that they would make fools of themselves. But a bunch of us had one, and everyone loved it.

One Valentine's Day, I had a sock hop. This really scared some of my more reserved friends. But I moved the furniture back and put on old Beatles and Rolling Stones tapes and everybody danced. Well, most people. The reason we could get as many as we did to dance was because everybody danced with their kids.

What are other things that some neighborhoods are doing? I've heard of a cooking co-op where three families take turns cooking each week and delivering food to the others. I've heard of a lot of eating co-ops where several people eat together two or three times a week, rotating houses. I've heard of women getting together not only to share child care, but to clean each other's houses.

But we don't have to just stick to work. You can plan fun things with friends like going camping together or having picnics. Some people start annual events, like a Fourth of July potluck or Christmas caroling. There's something about doing something with the same people year after year that makes it more special.

Personal

One of the biggest changes people seek is in their living patterns. It's not just college kids who share houses anymore. More and more adults of all ages are finding big houses and moving in together. Others are involved in the more formal planning of co-housing, where people buy land together and build several smaller houses around one community center—a community building with facilities for cooking and social events. Seniors are forming cooperatives so that they will have support without having to go to a nursing home. Many single women rent out a room in their home so they have extra money and don't feel so vulnerable.

Some of these things people do to save money. As is usually the case, when people are in economic straits, they often join together.

Service

A lot of people are creating community by joining together in their spare time to contribute to the well-being of the larger society.

Most of us know about people building homes for the poor through programs like Habitat for Humanity. People are even using their vacations to join programs that "make a difference." Every year, Arthur Frommer, the travel guide expert, puts out another edition of *New World of Travel*, a book featuring "alternative vacations that will change your life." New journals such as *Yes! A Journal of Positive Futures* and *Hope, Humanity Making a Difference* are featuring people getting together to make a difference.

Electronic Communities

I still refuse to think of anything on-line as a real community. But the question is, would those shy, introverted techies be forced to go out and talk if they didn't have their computers? Or would they just be more isolated?

You can always generate controversy by discussing community and computers. Some people absolutely love e-mail and say they communicate with their friends and relatives in other parts of the country much more. Others comment that now they don't even talk to the person in the office next door because they communicate on e-mail.

For some, communicating in electronic communities is a safe place to say things that they can't say to friends and families—the anonymity frees them, like talking to a stranger on a train. But don't we get enough anonymous talk as it is? I can't even keep up with my real friends, so why would I want to take time away from them to chat with strangers?

The challenge, it seems to me, is how to get the best of electronic community without having it eat up all of our time so that we have no time for anything else. One school reported that kids were coming to counselors because they were spending too much time on the Internet and it was disrupting the other parts of their lives.

For me, the Internet was mostly irritating and boring, until I got involved with the many social-action web sites on the World Wide

Web. Here is the hope for me—electronic democracy. As our insti-tutions get bigger and bigger and corporations take over more and more broadcasting stations, this may be a way to take back people's power. In the activist web sites you can not only get information on social and environmental issues, you can communicate directly to your senators and representatives by e-mail.

RE-CREATING DEMOCRACY

Ultimately, we won't change things in our world until we change the system of domination, until we re-create democracy. And we won't make a dent on the system of domination until people learn, really learn, how to be equals. And of course, you learn by experiencing. Unless we have that experience of day after day being treated with respect, affection, and dignity, we will accept our culture's idea that some people are better than others. We will accept people degrad-ing us or being rude to us, or not listening to us.

Unless we give people the feeling that their voice is important, that they have the right to speak out, we will not be able to fight the dominance of the corporate system and we will be unable to save either people or the planet.

It is the experience of community that leads to the re-creation of democracy.

12

LIVING IN COMMUNITY WITH THE EARTH

> As Okanagans our most essential responsibility is to
> learn to bond our whole individual selves and our
> communal selves to the land. Many of our ceremonies
> have been constructed for this. We join with the larger
> self, outward to the land, and rejoice in all that we are.
> We are this one part of Earth. Without this self we are
> not human: we yearn; we are incomplete. We cannot
> find joy because we need place in this sense to nurture
> and protect our family/community/self. The thing
> Okanagans fear worst of all is to be removed from the
> land that is their life and their spirit.
>
> —JEANNETTE ARMSTRONG

We have seen that community often springs up when people face a
threat together. What we must understand is that we *are* facing a
threat, together with the earth. If the earth is poisoned, so are we.
Maybe we need to think of ourselves and the earth as members of
one community. If we no longer see the earth as something totally
separate from us, perhaps we will consider its needs more often.
More and more people are starting to do that, in a field of behavioral
sciences some are calling ecopsychology. Ecopsychology explores
the idea that the earth is sick and needs us. We are sick and need
the earth. We are facing devastation together.

Once again, the needs of people and the planet are one. We are
beginning to understand that we are depressed and lonely because
we are cut off from other people. We also need to understand that
we are sick and despairing because we are cut off from the earth.

But it seems to have taken the mental health field a long time to realize this. One woman described her visits to a psychiatrist, where she talked about being depressed about the destruction of nature. The psychiatrist interpreted her depression as coming from a bad relationship with her mother. He couldn't conceive that she actually *was* depressed because the earth was dying.

So we don't just need community with other people, we also need community with nature. What does that mean? It means that just as we need to respect and care for people, hang out with people, work with people, communicate with people, we need to respect and care for nature, hang out with nature, work with nature, communicate with nature.

Often, one thing that brings us in closer touch with nature is a problem with our health. Many of us have changed our whole approach to nature when we have discovered that modern medicine does not always heal us.

NATURE AND HEALTH

Throughout human history, nature was central to people's health; now we are starting to pay attention to that again. Once again, I speak from experience. Although I have spent much more of my life in cafes reading than I have outdoors hiking, I still have come to see how important nature is to my health.

Several years ago, after five years of stress getting my doctorate, I got very sick with asthma. I had had a mild case of it before, stemming from allergies. But one summer it grew worse, and I needed to take more and more medication. I was afraid I would never really be able to breathe again without taking strong chemicals. I was very depressed, the most I had ever been.

Whenever I have a problem, I read lots of books and talk to lots of people. Luckily for me, there are a lot of books written on natural medicine. And because the leading naturopathic school in the country, Bastyr University, is located in Seattle, there are a lot of people to talk to about natural medicine.

If you have spent much time in the academic world, you have learned to scorn things that aren't anointed by the best and the brightest—people with Ph.D.s from Stanford or Harvard. Skepticism has its strong points, but too often it merely means that we have closed our minds. So I had never before considered trying anything that my conventional M.D. didn't recommend.

But when you are very sick, when the medications are making you feel even worse, you will try anything.

Often, you hear of an idea several times before you take action. I had heard people talk about going to a naturopath several times before, and one day I heard it again. A woman I worked with told me about how much a naturopath had helped her kids (once again, the power of stories). So I made an appointment.

Unfortunately, the naturopath's office was a little unnerving. There were few windows, and the color scheme was drab. I was really nervous, and I kept thinking, "What am I doing, coming to this quack?"

Before I had made the decision to go, I had, of course, met with my family doctor and a specialist several times. I remember one particular day—it was after visiting the specialist. I walked out of her office with a huge bag of medications, and the thought came to me, That's it. I am not going to take these medications. I am going to find another way.

I went back to my family doctor and told him I wanted to try something else. I am forever grateful for his response: "Well, it couldn't hurt," he said. The next day I made the appointment with the naturopath.

I worked with the "quack" for about six weeks, continuing to take my "real" medicine, which the specialist had told me I would need to take the rest of my life. It wasn't supposed to heal me, just control the symptoms.

Gradually, I got better, and I have never taken any asthma medication again, and that was almost fifteen years ago. I am so grateful, for I was so afraid, so depressed.

Trying out these new ideas wasn't easy for me. Those of us born in the forties will probably never be big risk takers. Our early years were affected by the war, and then, of course, came the conservatism of the fifties and our awe over dazzling new technologies. We trusted in authorities and in science, almost without question.

So it was hard for me to question modern medicine and turn to something that it scorned. But I read all I could. And I realized that the underlying philosophy of natural medicine made sense to me— why not work *with* nature to heal the body? Obviously, there was a healing force in the body; you could see it in the way your finger would heal after a cut.

And I liked the fact that there were so many approaches: herbs, vitamins, natural foods, massage, homeopathy. (I have always believed that there are several routes to the truth.) Homeopathy was the approach that I found most exciting. I discovered that in the nineteenth century, people I have admired, like Elizabeth Cady Stanton, Mark Twain, and Louisa May Alcott, had used homeopathy. Not only did the idea make sense, but the practice grew out of real experience (another approach to life that I value). The founder, Samuel Hahnemann, a nineteenth-century physician, developed homeopathy when he observed that taking quinine when you weren't sick produced malaria-like symptoms. Interesting, he thought, because quinine was what you took to get *over* malaria. So, he reasoned, maybe just a small portion of a substance stimulated your body to heal itself (similar to the way allergy therapy or vaccinations work). He started to experiment and his ideas spread. Today, growing numbers of people use homeopathy, including many mainstream physicians. It's used extensively in France, Germany, England, and India.

So after my experience with the naturopath and reading all I could, I found an M.D. who was also a homeopath—knowing that if homeopathy didn't work with me, my physician could turn to "regular" medicine. But she has never needed to.

Now, if I were in a bad car accident, I would want to go to the emergency room of a modern hospital. But I learned from my own experience that the conventional allopathic approach does not work for everything.

When your life has been saved, you become a believer. I have gone to my homeopathic physician, exclusively, all of these years. Homeopathy is also philosophically appealing. As with other natural approaches to medicine, it believes in a unity of the mind, body, and spirit. Part of the idea is that when we are out of balance, it shows up in a physical symptom. The symptom is a signal to you to do something to correct the imbalance. If that symptom is repressed, as it is by most conventional medicine, the disturbance just gets deeper. It refuses to go away. Many years later, the imbalance will show up in other ways, perhaps in emotional or mental disturbance. Further, homeopathy affirms the uniqueness of the authentic personality. You receive a "remedy," which is made of a natural substance, that fits your unique self. Your remedy fits your personal profile. But this remedy changes as you grow and change. You never just go to the doctor and get a standard antibiotic. You work with the physician finding full health as you become more and more your true self.

So the philosophy of homeopathy is congruent with the other answers I have found in my search for how to live my life—the idea that everything is connected, everything is one, and that we must learn to live in community with nature.

A SOCIETAL PROBLEM

The answer to my health problems wasn't just a personal one. Yes, personal stress may have helped bring on my asthma. But the stress of writing my dissertation was just the straw that broke the camel's back. Our bodies are assaulted all day long by toxins surrounding us. Once again, I learned of this through personal experience. This time it was the "sick building" syndrome. During a remodeling project in my college, a new carpet was installed. When I walked into the building after they had finished, my body reacted immediately. It wasn't only the horrible smell; my ears started to itch and my throat became scratchy. I had to leave right away.

I told everyone that something was wrong. But they all just said it was just the "new carpet" smell. Soon thereafter, secretaries in the building started getting weird physical symptoms and strange rashes. When they went to their doctors, the doctors asked if they had been around any toxic chemicals. These complaints weren't taken seriously either, because the *faculty* weren't complaining. Of course the faculty were in the building only a few hours a day, so their exposure was not as great. (The real reason these complaints were ignored is because the complainants were low-level women employees.)

It finally came to a head—a male administrator started getting symptoms—and the whole department moved out of the building until the carpet was removed. Now, several years later, the "sick building" syndrome is well established.

EXAMPLES FROM STUDY CIRCLES

Building community with nature is like building community in your neighborhood. It's not something grand, but the little day-to-day things that you do to use fewer resources. In simplicity circles one of the constant themes is inspecting every aspect of your life.

For example, there's one thing that is a symbol for me of our abuse of nature—a day-to-day example of how we have moved away from a simple product into one that is more complicated and uses more of the world's resources—it's our use of plastic bowls and lids.

Several times in my life I have succumbed to the lure of a sale on plastic bowls, thinking that now I could get my kitchen under control. The problem is, though, you can't store the lid *on* the bowl—your cupboards just aren't tall enough to stack them that way. So you have to store the lid separately. That means you can never find the lid because it is buried in a drawer full of lids. Which means your kitchen is even more out of control!

How were we bamboozled into thinking we needed plastic bowls and lids? Well, we thought they were better than using plastic wrap, because at least you were reusing something instead of throwing it in the garbage. But all along, there has been an old fashioned thing that worked even better, something that people are selling again: those little bowl covers that look like shower caps that we used in the past. They're perfect—they cost less, use fewer resources, and are easier to store. I've started giving them to people as gifts. You can get a package of six for a little over a dollar. I worry, though, that as time goes on, there will be no one who remembers them or recognizes them for what they are. My friends will wonder why I'm giving them these odd-sized shower caps!

Whenever you start to buy something that promises to change your life, think about the bowl covers. Here are some of the other things simplicity circle members recommend if you want to live in harmony with the earth.

Use Fewer Appliances

When you start understanding the need for a relationship with nature, you start cutting back on the appliances that you use. A lot of people give up their food processors, for a couple of reasons. One, it's irritating to clean the processor, but it's also because people enjoy chopping their vegetables by hand. It has more depth, more soul.

People use dishwashers, clothes dryers, bread makers, electric can openers, electric knives, electric popcorn makers, gas or electric-powered lawn mowers, hair dryers, and air conditioners less often. They increasingly use ceiling fans, brooms, dust mops, push mowers, clothes lines, clothes drying racks, and dish drying racks. Not only are brooms and such less complicated mechanisms, they use no energy and they involve you in a more intimate, real experience.

It's easier to be mindful of the moment when you are sweeping the floor than when you are vacuuming!

Limit Your Use of Water

Take short showers, install a water-saving shower head, don't leave the water running when you brush your teeth, put a bottle in your toilet tank to use less water per flush. Water your lawn at night. Better yet, since grass requires so much water, plow up your lawn and plant vegetables. Set up a gray-water system to catch the water you wash with to use on your garden.

Reduce Your Use of Paper

Reuse paper (reuse envelopes, make cards out of calendars, use the backs of scrap paper for notes), blow your nose on a handker-chief, use cloth kitchen towels and get rid of paper towels, carry your own cup with you so that you don't have to use paper cups, carry a cloth bag so that you don't have to use paper bags.

Drive Less

Driving less has so many benefits beyond the obvious ones of reducing pollution, reducing the use of oil, and saving money. When you decide to drive less, you find yourself living much more con-sciously. Before, you might have hopped in the car and driven to a shopping center when you wanted something. But when you are committed to driving less, you think about each trip more carefully, often deciding that you don't really need that thing you thought you wanted. So by reducing your driving, you save yourself more money and use up fewer of the world's resources. You get more time for the projects that are important to you and develop the ability to concen-trate for longer periods of time. It's so easy to just jump in the car and go that we often use the car as a way to escape from projects that need long periods of concentrated time. Maybe you'll write that book or really learn to play the guitar. Maybe you'll really get to all the things you've been wanting to do.

Of course, driving less helps build community. When you walk, you get to know your neighbors better. When you ask friends for rides, you get to know them better. When you take the bus you get to know your city better. When you walk or bike you feel better because you slow down, you think more, you get more exercise.

Eat Organically

Eating organically isn't only important for you, it is important for the farmers and earth. Our use of insecticides and pesticides poisons the people who apply them and makes the soil unfit for future farming.

Avoid Toxins

As the market for them grows, you can find more and more products made without toxic chemicals—toilet paper, sanitary napkins, cleaning materials, paint, beds, and on and on. You can buy clothes made from green cotton, a fabric made without chemicals, or install a shower head that takes the chlorine out of your shower water. There is a growing eco-building movement, and companies such as *Real Goods* or *Seventh Generation* have catalogues that feature products without toxins.

Save on Energy

Keep your heat low in the winter and the air conditioner set high in the summer. Wear natural fibers that breathe. Use compact florescent lights. They cost more initially, but they save energy and money in the long run. Lower the setting on your hot water heater. Don't use electric blankets. Not only do they use electricity, but research has found that the electrical fields are bad for you. Use flannel sheets and hot water bottles.

Reduce Your Consumption of Packaging

Buy in bulk to reduce the amount of packaging used. Work for laws similar to those some European countries have, where companies themselves are responsible for recycling their packaging.

Eat Less Beef

Consuming less beef is better for you. Furthermore, the grain used to feed cattle could instead be used to feed starving people and fewer trees would be cut down make grazing land for raising cattle.

Avoid Chloroflourocarbons

Chloroflourocarbons cause the hole in the ozone layer, increasing your risk of skin cancer. They are most often used in the manufacturing of fast food restaurants' cups and plates. Carry your own cup and ask the restaurant to not use Styrofoam.

Reduce the Use of Cleaning Products

Many of them are toxic, they cost money, and vinegar and baking soda will clean just about anything.

Avoid Disposables

Don't use disposable *anything* if you can help it—diapers, batteries, cameras, and on and on.

Always reduce, reuse, recycle or, as they said in the Depression, "Use it up, wear it out, make it do, or do without."

ALWAYS KEEP NATURE IN MIND

When you live with nature in mind, you may find some things to be more complex. But it can also become an exciting challenge and it will bring you a sense of meaning, a sense that you are contributing to your community.

Now, you might say, I don't have the time to do these things. Surprisingly, many of these things take less time in the long run, if you figure in the cost of repair and maintenance of appliances or if you take into account your improved health, with less time spent feeling sick or tired. But we have to quit seeing these things as a chore. Maybe if we thought of nature as alive, as a living thing, as community, we would be more willing to change our behavior. Taking care of nature would be a way of communicating lovingly with nature. Many of the toxic things we do, we do unconsciously. So each thing we do consciously is a way of communicating with nature, making nature part of ourselves.

Above all, find a way to get involved, find a way to fall in love with nature. Join an environmental organization. Go on nature hikes, join a bird-watchers group, clean up your park, join people restoring streams. When you work both with people and with nature, you will begin to feel complete, to feel that you have found real community. In everything we do, we need to keep nature in mind. Then caring for nature will become second nature.

PART 5

FIRE MAKERS

*I have spoken at times of a light in the soul, a light that is
uncreated and uncreatable . . . to the extent that we can deny
ourselves and turn away from created things, we shall find our
unity and blessing in that little spark in the soul, which neither
space nor time touches.*

—MEISTER ECKHART

And so, we come to the fire maker section, where we rekindle our spirit so that our own inner light shines more brightly. We try to learn to connect with a universal source of energy so that we feel fully alive. It involves rethinking our spiritual experiences, seeing spirituality in nature, and learning to live with a spirituality of everyday life.

13

RETHINKING SPIRITUALITY

i thank You God for most this amazing
day: for the leaping greenly spirits of trees
and a blue true dream of sky; and for everything
which is natural which is infinite which is yes

(i who have died am alive again today,
and this is the sun's birthday; this is the birth
day of life and of love and wings: and of the gay
great happening illimitably earth

how should tasting touching hearing seeing
breathing any—lifted from the no
of all nothing—human merely being
doubt unimaginable You?

—E. E. CUMMINGS

When I was in college, I memorized the first verse of the untitled
e. e. cummings poem quoted above. It was something that would
come to me on a glorious day and would help me to feel more deeply
what I was experiencing. It was only in the last few years that I read
the rest of the poem and realized that in the poet's mind this feeling
of joy is linked to a spiritual response to life. To have this sense of
ecstasy, the sense of aliveness that we are looking for, we need a
connection to a universal life force.

We can make all the changes we have talked about—cut back
on consumption, find our passion, create community—but even if
we do all those things, life can still be mundane and drab. We can
still suffer from the sleeping sickness of the soul. We want our days
to glow. We want to feel an energy bubbling up in us. We want to
feel as the poet does in his poem.

Most of us differentiate spirituality from religion. Spirituality is the larger category that embodies the experience of nature, art, community, love, creativity—all of these are elements of spirituality. It is a spirit of aliveness. Religion is tied to a creed, a body of principles—the Christian religion, the Jewish religion, the Hindu religion. Many of us have searched these religions looking for what Aldous Huxley called the perennial wisdom, the themes running through all religions.

But whether we choose spirituality or religion, we need a system of experiences and beliefs that is true to our own experience. Part of living fully is defining for ourselves what the spiritual life is. We must once again look at our own lives and discover what we already know.

We need to find our spiritual experiences in what moves us, not just look for them in church or an organized setting. For me, a spiritual experience must be something filled with joy and humor and aliveness, something that pierces the hypocrisy of our culture.

For me they have been: standing in a church basement in the South during the civil rights movement singing "We Shall Overcome"; sitting on a deserted beach watching the waves roll in; watching my daughter do her ballet exercises to Pachelbel's Canon in D; sitting in my garden surrounded by flowers; dancing to Beatles music.

I can remember no spiritual experiences in a regular church service. And I wonder what a spiritual experience in a church would be like? What would I want?

It would be like the e. e. cummings poem. It would connect, affirm, enliven, console.

It would need to connect you to something greater than yourself—an underlying life force that connects you to other people, animals, nature—the sacred circle of life.

It would affirm the individual's worth and dignity, affirm that everyone has a right to be who they are.

It would enliven, help you feel enthusiasm for life, a sense of energy.

It would enlighten—bring new light to your ideas, help you see through falsehoods and manipulation.

It would inspire—give you energy to move into the world and make a difference, to live in a compassionate, caring way, to work for justice.

It would embody a belief in an authentic self connected with a larger self, a belief that by listening to your inner voice, consulting the inner light, you can connect to the larger self. A belief that this inner voice will help you find your way.

Most of us want to live this way, but we have learned another view of reality. Charles Tart, in his book *Living the Mindful Life*, has people recite what he calls "The Western Creed":

> I believe in the material universe as the only and ultimate reality, a universe controlled by fixed physical laws and blind chance.
>
> I maintain that all ideas about God or gods, enlightened beings, prophets and saviors, or nonphysical beings or forces are superstitions and delusions. . . . Like the rest of life, my life and my consciousness have no objective purpose, meaning or destiny.

Tart has people repeat this creed, and he asks them how they feel. People say they feel depressed, sad, small, and closed in. They feel hopeless and despairing.

This, of course *is* our Western creed, what most of us have learned. Tart calls this "scientism, science distorted into an intolerant, fundamentalistic belief system." Most of us accepted this view of religious ideas out of a need to feel acceptable in the secular, academic world. Anything different branded you as some kind of a fool, an outsider, uncool.

But the rejection of religion started out in a healthy way as a questioning of narrow, orthodox beliefs, and of narrow minded, hypocritical churches that insulted people's intelligence. The church condemned people who questioned it as sinners, and failed to take stands against war or poverty. We needed to question these close-minded religions.

Some of us questioned churches on another basis—their support and advancement of patriarchy. For many of us the image of an old, white male God has been very harmful and very difficult to get over. That image is so strongly imprinted on our minds that it's hard for many of us to even explore religion.

We needed to question conventional religious views. But did we also need to learn to sneer at spirituality, to disdain the spiritual quest?

SEARCHING MY LIFE

Our early memories are often of having our spirit crushed, of experiencing the demeaning and belittling of our true selves. My first "religious" memory, which I'm sure laid the groundwork for my future questioning of authorities, was in the Pentecostal church—the holy rollers. It was when I was six. We were visiting Oklahoma, where my father's mother lived. She was a member of the church, and she clapped and shouted "Alleluia" right along with everyone else. Even though my parents didn't particularly like the church, they figured it wouldn't hurt me. So I went with her to church. One day, coming out of Sunday school, I suddenly felt very nauseated and weak. I told my grandmother, and much to my embarrassment, she told the minister. They hauled me up in front of the congregation and sat me down. Four or five men put their hands on my head and start praying out loud for me. After this went on for a while, they asked me how I felt. Well, I felt much worse, but I didn't want to tell them that—I didn't want to hurt their feelings or my grandmother's, and I certainly didn't want them to keep praying. But I hated to lie in church. This must have been one of my first moral dilemmas.

Well, I told them thank you very much, I felt much better, and I had to go. When I got home I went straight to bed and was diagnosed with measles the next day. Maybe it was lucky to have had this experience, because it taught me a lesson: their efforts were clearly ineffective. There was no way I could ever take fundamentalism very seriously after that. Although I didn't like lying, I learned to look out for my own best interests.

As a teenager, I attended the Methodist church and often had good ministers whose primary role was to make me think, but I had no spiritual experiences. My real spiritual experiences came from reading literature—from Thoreau, from women's novels.

Most of us broke completely from our childhood beliefs in college, but I went to college in the sixties and there were churches who taught me that religion involved social justice. Instead of sitting in church singing hymns, we walked picket lines and sang protest songs. I had experienced nothing like this in my suburban upbringing—either in the church or out of it, and I knew immediately that it was something I had been missing. I felt more alive than I ever had before.

My spiritual understanding continued to expand at the end of my college years when I was introduced to the Quakers, the Society of Friends. I was so moved when I learned about Quaker beliefs— that all people are of equal value, that there is "that of God in every person," that we must follow our inner light and sit in silence in order to hear that still small voice. These ideas continue to be central to me. Working with the American Friends Service Committee in the South during the sixties brought me a pivotal experience which I described earlier—my experience of the black church. I had never seen such aliveness, such spirit.

But the black culture was not my culture. I could learn from it, but not be a real part of it. Still, after experiencing it, I was dissatisfied with the Quakers. I wanted more life to my experience of worship. The silence of Quaker meeting was important to me, but I needed something more, something that stirred me like that black gospel music.

So I continued searching. I started reading novels by Jewish authors—Chaim Potok's *The Promise,* Michener's *The Source,* even the Kemelman mystery series, things like *The Friday the Rabbi Slept Late*. I was entranced by the feel of Judaism. I loved the sense of bringing the sacred into everyday life, the sense of history and justice, the intellectualism, the grappling with ideas, the community. When I was in my early thirties, I took a Jewish conversion course, which was something I had to talk my way into because Jews are not evangelical—a quality that made them even more appealing. But once again, I realized that I would never really be a part of the culture, so I did not convert. I was drawn to Judaism by what I understood as their consecration of daily life. I wanted that sense of celebration to be a part of my life.

I continued to search. Then I discovered that there was another element in Judaism that appealed to me, something I didn't fully understand at the time. I realized what it was when I joined my women's consciousness raising group in the early seventies. It was the focus on dealing with oppression. In my consciousness raising group I realized that I, too, was part of an oppressed group, and I realized that for me, resisting oppression must always be the core of any spiritual tradition—resisting my own oppression, others' oppression, and becoming aware of how *I* oppress others, how I oppress the earth. I realized that only when you are resisting oppression is there honesty and acceptance and community and laughter. And so, I discovered another element in my search for spirituality.

From the women's movement came the concept of *women's* spirituality, a viewpoint that helped me to see more clearly why I had not felt part of any earlier religious involvement. It sprang from the church's acceptance of sexism and patriarchy. With the women's movement came the questioning of everything, and the concept of a women's spirituality helped liberate me from the Christian church. I realized that I could never use the words of traditional Christianity, for Christianity had been spoiled for me.

It was spoiled for me when I was forced to lie in church. It was spoiled for me in high school when church was nothing more than a conventional rehash of society's mores. It was spoiled for me by the church's failure to guide me in life issues like choosing a career or a husband. It was spoiled for me in the blandness and conventionality of the Sunday service. Most of all, it was spoiled by its patriarchy, making it forever difficult for me to use the word *God*.

For me, the search is not over. As I review all that I have learned, I feel hopeful that I will continue to discover more. Yet, at the same time I feel that we must make peace with our own heritage. I can learn from other traditions, for instance, I can learn about the spirituality of nature from Native Americans, detachment from Taoism, meditation from Buddhism, but I am still an outsider. Can I reclaim anything of Christianity? Can I reinterpret it so that it is a source of energy and life for me?

One approach has drawn me. It is the theology of creation spirituality as expressed by Matthew Fox. It feels a little ironic to be excited by the words of a white male Catholic priest. Who would have thought? Of course, Fox is now an Episcopal priest because he was cast out of the Catholic church for being too unorthodox.

Matthew Fox is reclaiming Christianity for many people by making it broader than the *church* brand of Christianity. Just as I cannot adopt as my own the Native American spirituality or Judaism, I have also found that I cannot leave them out. For me, a spiritual approach must be one that connects us with all traditions. Creation spirituality, as Fox describes it, does this. It encompasses Judaism, Native American spirituality, Eastern philosophy, and the Goddess spirituality of feminists. Fox sees creation spirituality linked to native peoples everywhere—the Celtic people of Ireland, Scotland, Wales, and the Rhineland in Germany; the aboriginal people of Australia; the native people of Africa: "All these peoples had cosmology as the basis of their worship, prayer, economics, politics, and morality. All of them honored the artist in all persons. All expected the divine to burst out of anyplace at anytime. To see the world this way is to be creation-centered."

Creation spirituality not only incorporates the wisdom of people all over the world, but reclaims Christianity for those who are alienated from it: "Those who come into contact with it often become so ecstatic upon encountering this long-lost tradition, this heritage from their own Western roots, this treasure long-buried, that they want to move with it. They want the spirit that liberates their souls to be put to good use in liberating others. They want to set fire to the dry wood . . . that exists in lives, their communities, their institutions."

Fox describes creation spirituality in terms of four paths:

The Via Positiva: This path is the core of the spiritual life—it is awe, wonder, and delight. It is the path that brings us a feeling of *life*, the rekindling of our spirit, the sense of being on fire with excitement about life.

The Via Negativa: This path embraces our suffering as part of life. It doesn't try to ignore it or bury it as we do in our Prozac-addicted culture. It says that only by experiencing the darkness and letting go can we be transformed. It is the theme that has rescued so many alcoholics who find they must—in their words—"let go and let God." It is connected to the Taoist approach to life of not trying to control, dominate, or wrench life into the form we want, but respecting the river of life, giving yourself up to a flow of life. It is the antidote to our American approach that wants to dominate and master everything, to conquer, to bend things to our will. Anyone who has suffered knows that at a certain point, you have to give up and wait.

The Via Creativa: This is the path that says that what we are meant to be doing in life is creating—most of all, creating our lives.

The Via Transformativa: This path grows from all the rest. It is the path that says that none of the others will work if they do not encompass justice and celebration, which adds up to compassion. It says that we must all work for a relief of suffering, we must all work to combat injustice. But it is not a dour, grim approach. At the same time that we work for justice, we celebrate.

Together these paths bring us back to life and cure our sleeping sickness of the soul. Science has been our religion for a long time, but only the part of science that was devoted to controlling and mea-suring nature. We didn't learn about the views of Rachel Carson:

> A child's world is fresh and new and beautiful, full of
> wonder and excitement. It is our misfortune that for most
> of us that clear-eyed vision, that true instinct for what is
> beautiful and awe-inspiriting, is dimmed and even lost
> before we reach adulthood. If I had influence with the
> good fairy who is supposed to preside over the christening
> of all children I should ask that her gift to each child in
> the world be a sense of wonder so indestructible that it
> would last throughout life, as unfailing antidote against
> the boredom and disenchantments of later years, the
> sterile preoccupation with things that are artificial, the
> alienation from the sources of our strength.

And so, we are led back to concern about consumption. Even though every religion has always called for a detachment from riches, the post-war church, the one that so many of us grew up in, ignored this concern. There have always been some voices, of course. Rabbi Abraham Heschel links our obsession with consump-tion to our lack of awe and the church's dismissal of mysticism: "Forfeit your sense of awe, let your conceit diminish your ability to revere, and the universe becomes a marketplace for you."

In this view, our extreme consumption and lives of emptiness are directly linked to our affluence. Fox describes the experience of a priest who had been working with tribes in the Amazon. He asked him what he learned from them:

> "Joy. They experience more joy in a day than we do in a
> year. And they don't live as long or have as much as we
> do." Recently some African Americans who visited Africa
> for the first time were asked by the Africans there, "Why
> are you Americans so sad all the time?" Joy is lost when a
> cosmology is lost. Delight is reduced to the pseudo-

pleasures of buying and selling, winning and gossiping,
living vicariously in heroes and soap operas. Joy—a gift of
the spirit—is the starting point for the spiritual journey.

We need a change of consciousness, a metanoia, if we are to
cure our sleeping sickness of the soul. As Matthew Fox says, the
"key to ending apathy is to tackle despair, which you do by reminding people of their connection to divinity, their capacity to create
and co-create."

14

SPIRITUALITY AND NATURE

> The most beautiful thing we can experience is the mysterious.
>
> —ALBERT EINSTEIN

I have experienced joy—the joy of community, the joy of ideas, the joy of social protest. But what I have missed, I am beginning to realize, is a deep joy from nature. I have had inklings of this, but my background, growing up in the fifties and sixties, separated me from nature. Living in suburbia, I was surrounded with lawns and streets and cars. When we went out of town into nature, it was for a country *drive*. We never walked anywhere. Being an English major, I emulated the pseudo-intellectual, dissolute city people. Being a female in the fifties, I did hardly anything outside at all. I hated going camping because I didn't want to spend the whole weekend with my family—backyard barbecues were okay. That was pretty much it for nature. The whole fifties lifestyle of cars and movies and television was a barrier to involvement with nature. As I look back on it I am astounded to see how cut off from nature I was.

Only in the last few years have I begun to see what I have missed. I am beginning to realize that I will not live fully, that I will not be fully alive, unless I can experience a spiritual connection to nature. And, more important, unless people in our society feel this connection, we will not work to save either ourselves or the earth. If you don't love nature, if you don't feel intimately connected to it, you won't even notice as we destroy it.

Lately, as I have come to realize this, I have begun to feel differently, to see with different eyes. When I walk around the lake next to my home I am beginning to really look at it, to really sense the lake's presence. This growing spiritual connection to nature is one of the core reasons that people are attracted to voluntary simplicity.

As Willis Harmon, president of the Institute of Noetic Sciences, puts it, "A Native American elder summarized the native view in two short statements: 'Everything in the universe is alive' and 'We're all relatives.' How different from the modern white man's 'scientific' view of an essentially dead universe, operating according to fixed scientific laws, with the rest of the universe available for exploitation by humans in pursuit of economic ends."

Harmon is right. We must look to Native Americans to discover a spiritual connection to nature. In his book, *Look to the Mountain, An Ecology of Indigenous Education*, Gregory Cajete puts it this way:

> In all tribes, environmental understanding, environmental conservation, expressions of religion, and economic enterprise were fully integrated. Every step was a prayer, every waking moment was spent in communion with fellow humans; the natural world was a sacred pathway of knowledge, of learning and teaching the nature of being truly human, truly alive. It was a continuing process of developing one's capacity, one's potential, one's humanness, with the goal of reaching completion. Through striving for completion, each person gained an understanding of true relationship and purpose in life. When one views the world as a sacred place, a place that reflects a living process and way of being that goes beyond the human sense of experience, one deals with Nature in a very different way. It becomes a life and breath–charged experience.

GARDENING

My closest spiritual connection with nature has come when I am gardening. Alice Walker, in writing about black women's lives, real-ized the profoundness of gardening as she watched her mother work with her flowers: "I notice that it is only when my mother is working in her flowers that she is radiant, almost to the point of being invisible—except as Creator: hand and eye. She is involved in work her soul must have. Ordering the universe in the image of her personal conception of Beauty."

My whole life experience has taught me that the intellectual life is superior to the physical life, particularly the life of nature. So it wasn't until just a few years ago that I started gardening. I had always thought that the reason you gardened was to have flowers around, so it would look beautiful. I didn't realize that gardening was an end in itself.

In fact, I was astonished to see how much I loved weeding—it was almost a mystical experience. I would start weeding and become totally absorbed. Down on my knees among the tall flowers and plants, I felt different, I felt expanded. I wouldn't want to stop, even though I knew that, after all that bending, I probably wouldn't be able to walk the next day.

Gardening, growing something, whether it is in a pot on the window sill or a large backyard garden, is something that is available to everyone. Even if you can't visit the sea or hike in the mountains, you can find a way to garden. Eating your own tomatoes feeds your body and soul and brings you into connection with nature.

LEARNING FROM NATURE

And we can learn how to live from nature. More and more, nature is seen as a source of philosophy, a lamplight of guidance. Nature philosopher James Swan talks about certain themes in biology—the fact that the elements of nature cooperate with each other: the bee fertilizes the flowers, the droppings of the rabbit create rich soil for plants. Nature shows how we must learn to cooperate. Swan talks about plants finding their "niche" in nature, revealing to us our need to find our "niche," our passion.

In nature, there is no waste, everything is recycled, and so we learn that we too must recycle.

We learn that diversity is the nature of life, that everything is different, and thus we learn about the necessity to resist our society's march toward monoculture, our society's stupidity as well as cruelty in trying to crush people's ethnic cultures.

We learn how we should live from the flowers—that each flower grows from a seed, that you can't expect a daisy to emerge from a poppy seed. And so we learn that our authentic personality is present in us as a seed from the beginning.

We learn that we will recover from sorrow by watching the seasons in life, the continuous, unbroken cycle of life.

We learn equality and freedom from animals. As Walt Whitman says, "Not one is dissatisfied, not one is demented with the mania of owning things, Not one kneels to another, nor to his kind that lived thousands of years ago."

And more than anything, we have a respect for our natural, authentic self. We reject the artificial in our relationships with people as well as rejecting being surrounded by artificial things.

Learning that ecology is the basis of everything, that humans must learn to live in community with nature, is part of what Catholic theologian Thomas Berry describes as the Great Work. Every age, he says, has a Great Work. Ours is to redefine what it means to be human, to learn to be human within a community of nature, to create a new "ecozoic" period because never before has the earth faced what it faces today. Humans have altered its underlying chemical nature, and are sending its life into extinction. Unless we become a part of the Great Work, we will never feel the joy and exuberance of life again.

15

THE SPIRITUALITY OF EVERYDAY LIFE

Heaven is under our feet as well as over our heads.
—HENRY DAVID THOREAU

Some cultures embody spirituality in everything they do. In our culture, everything we do is a negation of spirituality. There is simply no room nor time for the spiritual life when you are preoccupied with getting ahead, making a profit, buying a new toy, plotting a takeover, managing your investment portfolio, answering the phone or shopping or watching television.

If our culture supported a spiritual view of the world, we could not live as we do, devoting ourselves to the profit motive and the accumulation of junk. Theodore Roszak puts it well: "The repression of the religious sensibilities in our culture over the past few centuries has been as much an adjunct of social and economic necessity as any act of class oppression or physical exploitation; it has been as mandatory for urban-industrial development as the accumulation of capital or the inculcation of factory discipline upon the working millions."

Even if we learn to change our thinking, we still must learn to change the way we live from day to day. Roszak says that we need to recover a "sacramental vision of being," to find the sacred in the profane. I think of this as the spirituality of everyday life. To live in small ways as if each day were sacred may be as important as trying to change our institutions and laws—without the change in daily behavior, there will be no energy for the bigger issues, because we simply won't care.

If we want to live with spirituality, to feel in touch with a universal life force, to feel joyful, how do we live day to day, hour to hour?

Once again, I talk from a personal point of view, although with reluctance because my efforts seem so inadequate. The realization of the meagerness of our spiritual lives is a testimony in itself to the state of our culture. And I suspect that I'm not alone. I suspect most people feel that their spiritual life is constantly pushed into the background as they are swept away by the frenzy of their lives.

How can we say that we have no time for a spiritual life? I remember those African-American women in the South, women who worked hours and hours scrubbing other people's floors, taking care of other people's kids, coming home late in the evening to begin again on their own floors and kids. These women did not neglect their spiritual lives. Seeing the dignity and radiance of these women made me feel ashamed of my own shallowness.

I want to change this, and I think that one way to change it is to speak honestly about it. We have to tell the truth about our lives.

HONESTY

In fact, I must speak honestly, because honesty is the core of my spiritual life. Through the years I have learned that my strongest imperative is to be honest. Whenever I have gone against it, life has gone badly. I have to be honest with myself and to others. Without honesty, we cannot develop the authentic self that is our gateway into experiencing life with depth. Listening to the source of our honesty, the inner voice, is connecting with the larger source of honesty—the universal spirit.

First, I must be honest to myself. As Virginia Woolf said, "If you do not tell the truth about yourself you cannot tell it about other people."

Being honest with yourself isn't easy. Too often we follow only our cultural scripts about who we should be, how we should act. So questioning is part of being honest. Critical thinking is part of being honest. We are searching for the truth.

People may not think of honesty as part of spirituality, but it is essential. What you believe must feel true to you, it can't contradict your experience, your feelings, the rest of your beliefs. Being honest with yourself is listening to that inner voice, the voice that seems to come from a larger source, which some call God and some call the collective unconscious. Being honest with yourself is sitting and waiting to hear what that inner voice tells you, and waiting some more. Every time I have ignored the inner voice, I have taken the wrong path.

I've always loved the story involving the founder of Pennsylvania and Quaker, William Penn. A man who had converted to Quakerism wore a sword as part of his uniform. Since Quakers are pacifists, the man asked William Penn how long he should keep wearing his sword. Penn told the man, as long as he could. What Penn meant was that everything we do must spring from a deep prompting, rather than from external cues.

Remember, we are surrounded by messages to conform. The only way to resist is to be true to that inner voice.

SILENCE

Half an hour's meditation is essential except when you are very busy. Then a full hour is needed.
—FRANCIS DE SALES

The only way to hear this inner voice is to sit and be silent at some time in your day. We need silence for a lot of reasons. We need silence to try to understand who we are, to develop our true selves, to be honest with ourselves. We need silence to stay open to the inner voice, the voice of the universal spirit.

We need silence in the evening in order to think through our day so that we will know what we felt, what we observed. Things go so fast, we are often not aware of what we are really feeling. As a result we are vulnerable to manipulation. Unless we take time to think about our experiences, they stay on the surface and don't become a part of our inner wisdom.

We need to sit in silence in the morning to process what we thought about the night before, to think about our feelings and dreams and what they meant. We need silence in the morning to sort through how we will live that day so we will be clear and not easily dragged off track.

So, I begin the day with silence. It's never as long as I would like, because of course I am fighting with being too busy like everyone else. I try to observe my five-minute rule: when I feel resistant to doing something I have committed myself to—like sitting in silence—I must do it every single day, for at least five minutes. That sounds paltry, but with that rule, I do *something*. When I start out by doing something for five minutes, I usually wind up doing it longer.

I begin my silence by just sitting and letting my mind wander wherever it wants to. There's even a practical side to this, because I often think about things that I need to remember. It's as if I have something within me that is ordering my inner self. Periodically, something will pop up that I had totally forgotten about—it's my own inner calendar. So even if you find yourself going over a list of things to do at the beginning of your silence, that's okay. I feel like this is my chance to think through things, to sift through my plans, and see things more clearly. I can begin to see which plans are not important, which ones are a waste of my energy because I am only doing them to meet others' expectations, only doing them because I was too unclear to say no.

I use silence to make decisions. I will sit and imagine how each decision feels. If a decision brings a sense of dread, I decide against it. If I feel a sense of peace, a sense of completeness, a sense of energy, I decide for it. I could not decide without the silence.

Often I will read a short passage, a poem or a quote from Thoreau. And again, just sit and see what comes to me. I like to have a pencil and paper with me, or else the thought that comes will be totally gone.

Finally, I have developed four things that I do each time I sit in silence. I ask to remain open to the universal spirit of life; I focus on what I feel grateful about; I ask for help for my son and my sister, who have had difficult lives; and I ask for guidance in my life's work. This has become my ritual. Each time I focus on these four areas, the experience of sitting in silence becomes a deeper one.

STUDY

Studying is also a part of my spiritual life. This is where I feel energy radiate through me. Everything I read and think about has to do with spirituality, because everything is related to that essential question: How can I be fully alive? I look at everything with that question in mind. When I read I am looking for the answers that will help me break free of my particular cultural script, break free of the cultural restraints that are keeping me from living fully. I study events in my day to see what I can learn from them, to see what meaning emerges in terms of my life values.

Others may not put as much emphasis on study as I do, because studying is part of who I am. It's not everyone's path. Actually, studying *is* a part of everyone's path, but not studying in the sense that our schools embody it. Studying involves elements other than just reading and writing. Studying is a form of disciplined searching, and each person can develop their own discipline, the approach that helps them find meaning.

Studying is ultimately a search for our own truth, and we each search for it in our own way. My son is an artist, and reading has never been his way. But when we discuss issues about life, I am amazed at what he has learned merely from living and feeling and reflecting, from observing and paying attention. Even though he went to school, his real schooling was closer to the Native American's experience of learning—sitting and observing and then asking what you have learned. Our culture is self-righteous about the printed word, making us feel that people with an oral tradition have no wisdom.

Ironically, as a nation we read less and less, so we have no cause to be superior about the superiority of reading. Nonetheless, everyone needs to sit down to study something—whether it is reading material or just their own experiences—in order to counteract the messages of consumerism and conformity that we are getting all day.

MINDFULNESS

What all this is about, remember, is trying to feel fully alive, to keep ourselves and the earth alive. And, as Thoreau was to say in so many ways, that means living fully in the present. For most of us, our attention is constantly diverted. We're rarely aware of what we are doing.

Take food. Food is probably one of the best symbols of our American way of life. Food is meant to nourish us, but it is also meant to be enjoyed. And the only way you can enjoy it is to pay attention to your eating. But we never do that. Our contribution to world cuisine is fast food. What does it mean to have drive-through windows to get our food? We have invented food that can be eaten with one hand while we're doing something else. It's pathological. We're not tasting the food; we're not getting any real pleasure or even nourishment out of it. And with all the chemicals and petroleum involved in our food production, our way of eating is destroying the planet as well. In other words, we're trashing the planet for something we are not even enjoying.

So one way of being mindful is paying attention to and savoring what you eat. When you eat, focus on enjoying eating.

In living mindfully, we pay attention to whatever we're doing and "suck out all the marrow," as Thoreau said. We become deeply absorbed in what we are doing, appreciating the people we are with, being conscious of the wind on our face. It means paying attention to what you are doing, and not doing ten things at once. Taking the time to notice, slowing down, sitting peacefully, and just being.

TIME ANXIETY

Being mindful is hard for us because we are always anxious about time. Just as we never feel we have enough money, we never have enough time. In fact, maybe it's because we feel we don't have enough money that we feel that we don't have enough time. Since we measure everything in terms of money, that sense of scarcity pervades our whole life. Learning that we have enough—money, time, love—may be our most important lesson.

Even when we eliminate the apparent obstacles of working and consuming too much, we still have trouble relaxing and enjoying the present moment. So the problem is not just the scarcity of time, it's our attitude toward time. That little voice always creeps in, You'd better hurry, you've got a lot to do, you're not getting enough done, time is running out. What does this mean in terms of feeling alive? Surely, if things keep on this way, when we come to die, we will discover that we have not lived.

We live in constant anticipation of the future, regret and guilt over the past: we can hardly wait for the weekend, for summer vacation, for the kids to be grown up, until retirement. We might as well say, "I can hardly wait until I die."

In the past I read books that told how to get more done during the day, how to find that extra hour so you could study French or learn photography. I would try to do as many things as I could at one time. Now I focus on doing less and slowing down. I try to stop rushing, to practice mindfulness, to practice meditation. I keep working at it, but still I have that nagging feeling—hurry, hurry.

We get upset at everything that gets in our way. We yell at other drivers, using language that shocks us. We switch checkout lanes in the grocery stores, we click through TV shows, we hurry our kids. Once, in a frantic effort to get ready for a birthday party for my kids, I tried to blow up balloons while I was driving.

Is it the universe's revenge? We, who have ruined the earth's resources, have had our only true resource, time, ruined for us. We are a caricature of a whirling dervish. We have made a mockery of so many of the world's spiritual traditions—all of which warn against excessive greed—that we've been set spinning, unable to stop and enjoy life.

I try not to rush and to move slowly as I clean the kitchen. But my husband, who doesn't think about these issues as much as I do, who is still in a traditional job, undergoes a personality change every Monday morning—starting to frown, starting to be impatient, intent on beating the clock. As Thoreau said, "As if we could kill time without injuring eternity." And we *are* killing time. That used to mean just sitting around, but now, in our frenzied activity, we really are killing time. So much of our time is spent in ways that kill our spirit, our capacity to enjoy the moment, to experience the depth of the moment. Americans, who are so egocentric, think we have built the best possible civilization, but we have no time to enjoy it.

And why? Because time has become money. What a joke. We value money above all. We measure our most precious commodity, time, in terms of money, and find that we can't enjoy time at all. A Faustian bargain. You want to have all the money in the world? Okay, you can have money, but no time to enjoy life.

Sometimes I will go into my husband's study as he sits there writing on his computer and say to him, "Well, this is it! This is your life! It's probably not going to get any better!" How else can I remind him, and myself, to take time seriously, to not let it slip away.

MOVING SLOWLY

I love a broad margin to my life. Sometimes in a summer morning, having taken my accustomed bath, I sat in my sunny doorway from sunrise to noon, rapt in a revery, amidst the pines and hickories and sumachs, in undisturbed solitude and stillness. . . . I grew in those seasons like corn in the night, and they were far better than any work of the hands would have bee.They were

not time subtracted from my life, but so much over and
above my usual allowance.
> —HENRY DAVID THOREAU

Why should we live with such hurry and waste of life?
> —HENRY DAVID THOREAU

To live mindfully, to appreciate your time, you have to move
slowly. There's nothing more difficult for Americans, and we have
gotten worse in the last twenty years. Court reporters find that we talk
faster. We walk faster, our movies are faster. MTV is the perfect
example. Just as you start to focus on an image, the camera moves on.

What is this addiction to stimulation? Sometimes I feel
addicted to my own adrenaline. If I'm not rushing, feeling pressured,
I feel like I'm missing something. Is this the only way we can feel
alive now—by rushing? Are we mistaking the rush of caffeine for a
feeling of vitality? Does rushing make us feel like we are doing
something important, that we are important people? Are we all
engaged in such meaningless work that we can only feel important
if we feel pressured? Do we have to convince ourselves and others of
the importance of our work to justify our existence?

Here is where mindfulness comes in. You must pay attention to
your speed and consciously slow down. Maybe make that your
mantra—slow down—saying it very slowly.

Rushing as we do means that things are always going wrong.
You always drop things and break something and have to clean up,
so it takes longer anyway. It's like speeding and getting stopped by
the police: you lose all that time you were trying to gain.

And of course, in our rushing, we have no time to talk with people, so we get lonelier and lonelier.

In rushing, we have no time for reflection, no time to notice
what is going on around us. We can't reflect on warning signals that
come to us—warning signals such as early signs that something is
wrong with our health. Signs that you are starting to drive too fast.
For instance, whenever I have a near miss in my car, I always say to

myself, Ahh, a message from the universe, and I slow down and become more careful in my driving.

Once I walked in on a man in the process of robbing my house. On my walk up to the door I had noticed several little things I later realized should have told me what was happening. But I ignored them. I escaped unharmed, but once again I thought to myself, You ignored the signs. You didn't pay attention.

When we rush, we are much more likely to consume because we are ignoring the little voice asking us if we really need this new thing. Impulse buying is what corporations depend on.

I think that little voice is always there speaking to us, telling us the right thing to do, but we ignore it because we are rushing and have no time to listen.

GRATITUDE

This is what I would like to feel more than anything. Gratitude. How else can you really enjoy your life? To feel gratitude is to look at everything in your life and appreciate it, be aware of it, pay attention to it. Our lifestyle, of course, engenders discontent and resentment. Because *more* is always better, you can never be satisfied with what you have. Because commercials are constantly showing us ecstatically happy people with lots of stuff, we always feel that we're just not quite making it. Then, when we see how much money rich people have, we feel envious. All of these feelings make you discontent with your life, causing you to fail to be grateful for what you do have.

So each morning, I consciously think about what I am grateful for and repeat e. e. cummings's words to myself:

> i thank You God most for this amazing
> day: for the leaping greenly spirits of trees
> and a blue true dream of sky; and for everything
> which is natural which is infinite which is yes

PART 6

TORCH BEARERS

CREATING A NEW SOCIETY

I've said several times that to change our lives we need both to change the way we think about the world and to change those parts of the world that help make us think that way.
—PHILIP SLATER

Most of this book is devoted to individual change. Individual change is necessary, but it is never enough. There also needs to be institutional change. As Slater says, "We need both to change the way we think about the world and to change those parts of the world that help make us think that way." We need to develop both belief systems and structures.

We need structures and policies that encourage caring and discourage greediness and prohibit the devastation of life. As torch bearers, we examine the issues of wealth and equality, and see what significance they have for building a society that values people and the planet. We look at structural changes that will encourage caring and equity and discourage destruction and injustice. Finally, because institutional changes take time, and we all want our lives to improve as soon as possible, we look at examples of individual workplace changes.

As torch bearers, having made changes in our own lives, we move out into the broader society to make changes there—to pass the torch.

16

WHAT'S WRONG WITH WEALTH

> Someday our grandchildren will very likely look back at the individual, selfish control of the wealth of the world by a small elite the same way we view slavery today.
>
> —Corinne McLaughlin
> and Gordon Davidson

> By poverty is meant enough money to live upon. That is, you must earn enough to be independent of any other human being and to buy that modicum of health, leisure, knowledge and so on that is needed for the full development of body and mind. But no more. Not a penny more.
>
> —Virginia Woolf

I was getting dressed one morning and half listening to a TV interview with a Swedish businessman when one of his comments caught my ear. "When you have heavy taxes, it takes away the desire to get rich, and then you start focusing on things that are more important than money. You care about other things than just getting ahead."

That stopped me in my tracks. What a novel, and very un-American idea! I was almost surprised it made it on the air for every red-blooded American to hear.

And then, some time later, I heard a somewhat similar story. It was told by a reporter who had been stationed in Russia for many years. She said that under communism, when ordinary people didn't have much chance for making a lot of money, they had long dinners and sat around all evening laughing and talking. After the fall of communism, there was no more sitting around after dinner because everybody felt they needed to get out and hustle.

It appears that the chance of acquiring wealth can negatively affect people's behavior. Yet that is a very difficult thing to accept. At some level most of us believe that individual wealth is a positive good. Now, if you asked people if they thought money brings happiness, many would say no. They would say that things like love and meaning make you happy. But if you then ask people if they would like to win the lottery, they will say yes. Even though research shows that winning the lottery doesn't increase happiness—and indeed, may decrease it—at some level we all think that we would be happier with more money. It is a belief that seems to be at the root of our American character. So one of the most important things we can do is begin to understand the way wealth affects us.

HOW WEALTH HARMS SOCIETY

The Rich Steal from the Poor

If you saw someone go up to a homeless man on the streets and grab the money out of his hat on the sidewalk, you would be incensed. Of course, this really is what is happening.

Concentrated wealth always steals from the poor, in many ways:

The rich make large profits because they do not pay workers well.

When products cost too much, the consumer goes into debt, particularly on necessities like medications.

When you decrease the tax burden for the rich, as we have done in the last twenty years, there is less money for social welfare, like infant nutrition programs or school breakfast subsidies.

We might get upset about someone grabbing from a poor man sitting on the street, but we don't realize that this is happening all of the time.

Gaps in Wealth Undermine Democracy

Great gaps in wealth undermine democracy because they give the rich more say in government. Our elected officials are beholden to contributions from corporations, so we have "the best Congress money can buy."

Gaps in wealth keep people quiet. A *New York Times* poll found that people said they were much less likely to speak up than they were a few years ago because they were afraid they would lose their jobs, and few had a nest egg to fall back on.

It's not just a fear of poverty that keeps people quiet, it's also the *possibility* of wealth that shuts people's mouths. Since we still have the myth in this country that it is possible for anyone to achieve great wealth, we all think we will have our shot if we don't rock the boat. We keep quiet in order to get ahead.

Most media are owned be a handful of corporate conglomerates, so a small group of people control the information we receive—and the worldview that is presented.

When there are great gaps in wealth, it is difficult for the wealthy to truly understand the problems society faces because they are not experiencing them. George Bush was a good example. When his handlers sent him to the supermarket to encourage people to spend money, he had never seen an automatic bar-code checker. Rich people who buy their own water, put in a security system, live away from the inner city have no knowledge of what is really going on in the real world. Moreover, they think that because they have always bought themselves out of things, they can keep doing it. I've heard more than one person talk about finding another planet for us to go to rather than working to change our profligate ways now.

The Desire for Extreme Wealth Produces Crime

We always think of the poor committing crimes for money: robbing banks, writing bad checks, dealing drugs. White collar crime is motivated for the desire for money just as crime in the streets is.

Think of the crimes of high finance—from the embezzlement of funds to the shady dealings of the Milkens and the Boeskies.

Gaps in Wealth Cause Violence

There's violence on the street, violence when someone breaks into your home, and the threat of violence in riots and sabotage. An imbalance of wealth in society simply causes envy and rage. And the poor of society have no other way to strike back. Eventually we are all targets of violence and then violence becomes the law of the land.

For instance, consider concern over increasing violence among youth. Our tendency is to blame lack of parental supervision; we are even arresting parents for their supposed neglect. But the real cause appears to be related to economics. Murder reached an all-time high during the Depression with 9.7 homicides per 100,000 population. Never has murder in this country reached a comparable level until today. Youth homicides number ten per 100,000. And look at which youths are committing the crimes: in 1993, thirty-one California counties had no youth homicides. In central Los Angeles, there were two hundred. The level of wealth in the counties was the main difference.

Wealth Causes Wars

Wealth also causes another kind of violence. Why did we go to war in the Persian Gulf? Because of oil, because oil brings people wealth.

We also needed to try out those expensive weapons. Somebody was getting wealthy building weapons.

Wealth Wastes Money

The money that we could be spending on schools, support for the arts, and reclamation of the environment is spent instead on police, prisons, and the military. Almost all of this money is spent to protect the interests of wealth. The police and the prisons protect the wealthy at home and our military protects their interests abroad.

Wealth Increases Consumption

Americans comprise 5 percent of the world's population and consume 30 percent of its resources. A person in the United States causes one hundred times more damage to the global environment than a person in a poor country. When you have money, you tend to spend it.

HOW WEALTH HARMS INDIVIDUALS

All of society is harmed by extreme wealth and the attempt to become wealthy. But for people to really understand the harm of extreme wealth, they need to understand how it harms the individual. Now, just as some people are immune to the flu even when everyone around them is coughing, some rich people are immune to the negative consequences of extreme wealth. By and large, though, extreme wealth harms the individual.

This is not, of course, to argue for extreme poverty. The argument is for a lifestyle that allows people to have enough, but not so much that it damages their own lives, others' lives, and the life of the planet. One of the biggest challenges we face today is determining just how much is enough.

Wealth Doesn't Guarantee Happiness

Studies show that wealth increases happiness for only one group—the poor. What seems to matter, after having enough money for food and shelter, is satisfaction with your income, and people with high incomes are not much more satisfied with their incomes than people with lower incomes.

In his book *The Pursuit of Happiness*, David Myers shows how an increasing affluence in this country has not brought more happiness. Our buying power has doubled since the 1950s, but certainly not our happiness quotient. We have twice as many cars and TVs than we did in the early sixties, but we are certainly not twice as happy.

Wealth Decreases Creativity

When you have money, you tend to spend it rather than doing other more creative things. Spending time shopping is time subtracted from reading, or meditating, or helping the poor. It would be very difficult to argue that shopping helps people become wise and caring.

Inherited wealth often makes it hard for a person to seriously commit to a profession, so there is a missed sense of achievement or of meeting challenges. Too often rich children have little motivation to achieve. Even Bill Gates, rated the richest man in the world for several years, recognizes this: he's said he will give away his fortune like Andrew Carnegie rather than burden his kids with it. (We'll see.)

Wealth Undermines Integrity

To become wealthy, a person often sacrifices values about fairness and justice. How many times have we read about a company putting profits before people, even in life and death matters. Insurance companies turn down claims for treatment that could save a life. Tobacco companies add extra nicotine to addict people to cigarettes. When you are a CEO of those companies, at some level you know that people are being hurt as you profit.

Wealth Destroys Trust

An imbalance in wealth destroys trust among people. When you're rich, you're suspicious of the poor, worried that they might try to take your money as they have in the past when they robbed or mugged you. When you are poor, you're suspicious of the rich, worried that they will try to take your money from you as they have in the past when they underpaid you or charged you too much for their products. Everyone is suspicious about being ripped off.

Wealth Cuts You Off from Life

When you have a lot of money, it's hard to live fully, because you can always buy yourself out of your problems. You purchase comfort and convenience rather than experience discomfort and challenge. You miss a lot of life.

Wealth Makes You Sick

Even though rich people may not be starving, they more often have diseases like cancer and heart problems; diseases caused by stress and eating a diet rich in sugar and animal fats.

WHAT CAN BE DONE?

So it seems that wealth can ruin our community lives, our personal lives, and the life of the planet. It is both having wealth and the possibility of getting wealth that seems to undermine us. The answer seems to be to make it impossible for people to attain extreme wealth. Being very rich just shouldn't be an option, because as long as it is, most people will focus on acquiring wealth as their life goal.

When little kids come into a room with delicate valuables, what do you do? You don't let them break things, you put them away and find something more interesting for them to do. You don't keep yelling at them, "No, don't touch that!"

We need to take away the possibility of attaining great wealth and give people more interesting things to do—we need to create structures that limit accumulation of great wealth.

17

STRUCTURAL CHANGES

It is a mistake—as so many over-centralized socialist societies have discovered—to try to eliminate money as an incentive. Money is one incentive among many, and has its place. But to put no limits on the impulse to accumulate money obsessively is as destructive as to place no limits on the impulse to commit violence. A viable democratic society needs a ceiling and a floor with regard to the distribution of wealth and assets.

—PHILIP SLATER

CREATING A NEW CULTURAL VISION

We want to create a society in which the quality of life both for people and for the planet are more important than the attainment of wealth. In an earlier chapter, we talked about moving from an egocentric ethic in which people are motivated by greed to an ecocentric ethic that values people and the planet. We need to create a belief system that makes the welfare of people and the planet a higher priority than the belief in the right of a few people to get rich. What are the characteristics of an ecocentric society?

Caring

We want to create a society that is caring. Lack of caring is at the root of the people's despair and the planet's devastation. When you care for people and the planet, you won't sell them down the road. We have seen that in order to be caring, we need to experience caring. So we need structural changes that allow people to behave in a caring way.

Security

As long as people feel insecure about their ability to survive, they will stay in the old system of striving for more. As long as people are worried that they'll be left behind, they'll keep on the treadmill of work and spend. We need structural changes that give people security.

Equality

Sometimes, when I'm driving on a freeway and marvel at the fact that we're all out there careening along without crashing into each other, I see our traffic system as a metaphor for life. We're pretty much following the rules, and we usually reach our destination without an accident. The reason? Of course there are the structures of licenses, laws, and punishments, but more important is the fact that on the highway, we're all pretty much equal. If someone runs into me, it will probably hurt him or her as much as it will hurt me.

It's easy to see that inequality hurts people, but perhaps it is the system of hierarchy and dominance that is at the root of our environmental problems—when dominance over people is acceptable, we feel it's acceptable to dominate and exploit the planet.

Participatory Democracy

As Philip Slater shows in his book, *A Dream Deferred*, democracy is the only system that is flexible enough to manage our problems. All theories about change show that change does not succeed unless there is participation by people who are affected. We need structures that encourage participation.

Critical Thinking

People need access to accurate information and a way to talk over what they have learned in order to understand what is in their long-term best interest. We need systems that encourage critical thinking.

CONCRETE PROPOSALS FOR A NEW SOCIETY

Finding structures that encourage caring, security, equality, democracy, and critical thinking requires a lot of creativity, talking, and study. I am going to describe some of the solutions that have seemed exciting and important to simplicity circle members. This list is not comprehensive and is meant mainly to spark conversations. There will be no change without dialogue and discussion. Giving consideration to some of these ideas is a good start.

Develop a New Standard of Economic Health

In trying to develop a new vision of societal well-being, we need to have a new way to measure what is going on in the economy and society.

The current measurement used by the government and academics, the Gross Domestic Product (which used to be the Gross National Product before multinational organizations made that an inaccurate measure), reflects that we are doing well. Yet 70 percent of the American public feels unhopeful about the future.

Many groups are urging our government to adopt a different way of measuring progress. For instance, some recommend that we adopt a standard called the Genuine Progress Indicator, a measurement that would more accurately reflect reality. Put simply, the GDP measures all money that changes hands. If money is involved, the GDP goes up. That means negative activities as well as positive activities make our economy look like it's growing.

Even though the Exxon *Valdez* oil spill was bad, it boosted the GDP. Crime is a great booster because of a huge crime-prevention industry. Pollution can count twice—once as a part of an industry that produced it and another as part of an industry to clean it up.

If no money changes hands, the activity is ignored: the unpaid work of caring for family and friends or volunteering in community projects isn't counted, so it is not valued.

The GPI, the Genuine Progress Indicator, includes factors ignored by conventional measurements, such as the value of home and community work. Things such as pollution and crime, resource depletion and degradation of the habitat are included as the negatives that they truly are.

Not surprisingly, the GPI shows things are getting worse. It shows an upward curve from the early fifties until about 1970, and then a decline of about 45 percent to the present. What that means is that costs of our economic activities are starting to outweigh the benefits.

If we begin to see things in more realistic terms, we can more easily argue for the following changes.

Develop New Kinds of Taxation

Taxation brings in money to run the government, but it also sets policy. The way we tax affects people's behavior. For instance, when people advocate a "sin" tax, they are trying to discourage things like smoking by making cigarettes very expensive.

Reducing Consumption through Taxation

Although there are a variety of policies that could reduce consumption, some argue that the only way to get people to quit using up resources is to price things out of range through taxation. Thus in Denmark, the tax markup on cars is so high that people buy fewer cars. The taxes that are collected can be used to provide public transportation.

In Europe as a whole, there is a growing movement advocating *green* taxes or ecological tax reform. Basically, green taxes cut income taxes and payroll taxes and, at the same time, tax activities that create pollution and use up natural resources.

This approach is also popular with the public because it reduces unemployment: by lowering payroll taxes, companies can afford to hire more people. By lowering income taxes, more people can afford to work part time—further helping unemployment by spreading the jobs around.

What we would really be doing with green taxes is reflecting the *true* costs of production: the costs of pollution and the use of resources. In the long run, someone pays for pollution, and we know who that is.

Limiting Wealth Accumulation

If we are thinking of true well-being and health, our earlier discussion on the negative consequences of wealth seems to indicate that we must limit the ability to acquire great wealth.

Economist Juliet Schor, author of *The Overworked American*, advocates a more simple and fair tax system: there should be more exemptions for low-income people and higher taxes for the rich. There should be more taxes on corporations and higher inheritance taxes.

Create Security by Setting a Minimum Level of Support

As long as people have both the possibility of great wealth or the possibility of dire poverty, the desire for more will dominate us. We not only need to set an upper limit on wealth, but a lower limit. Europe is beginning to discuss what it calls a Basic Income Grant (BIG) where everyone would receive a minimum income from the government that would allow them to live modestly. It would allow people to periodically opt out of the labor market to pursue studies, raise children, create their own business, or live as artists.

Ironically, we want to cut the welfare rolls and promote workfare at a time when there just are not enough jobs to go around. In fact, when unemployment drops, the stock market often takes a dive, because the market worries that low unemployment will cause inflation causing interest rates to rise. Perhaps it will be Wall Street who supports a basic income grant.

Because we have so many problems of addiction and mental illness, giving money outright to people might not be possible. However, we can give people the things they need money for in the first place: food to eat, a place to live, and basic medical care. Access to these necessities should be a right.

Provide Work

Few politicians are going to recommend a basic income grant. But if we don't do that, then we had better guarantee people jobs. But is this possible? Our jobs are disappearing as companies continue to automate and transport jobs overseas.

One of the most often-mentioned ways to provide more work is to reduce the work week and spread jobs around. This can be done in a way that both employees and employers benefit.

For instance, some companies find that people will accept a lower salary if their hourly wage goes up. Since productivity tends to rise when people work shorter hours, both the people and the company would benefit: there would be higher productivity for the company and a higher hourly wage for the people.

Juliet Schor found that only 23 percent of adults say that if they had enough income to live comfortably, they would prefer to work full-time. Schor advocates tax policies that would induce employers to offer a variety of options such as trading income for time off, job-sharing, and the upgrading of part-time work. She recommends policies that would prohibit mandatory overtime, policies that would replace overtime pay with comp time (including salaried workers), and policies giving all American workers a guaranteed four week vacation. All of these policies would create more jobs and give overworked Americans a chance to have a full life.

Jeremy Rifkin suggests taxing companies with high profits and giving grants to nonprofit organizations to hire people to expand their work. With this plan, we need not expand the government and we could ensure quality of work by giving grants only to agencies that have proven their effectiveness over the years. This plan would employ more people and attack our social problems at the same time.

Cut Back on Defense Spending

One way to find more money to make these changes is to cut back on defense spending. It not only would generate a great deal of money, but the defense industry is one of the biggest polluters—war is the biggest polluter of all.

Reform Campaign Financing

None of the above will be accomplished until our Congress is freed from its bondage to corporations. Both parties are held hostage by corporate contributions.

Part of election reform is finding ways to increase voter turnout. Some advocate making voting mandatory as it is in Australia, where, if you fail to vote, you are fined. There should be universal registration, which could be done by the post office or the IRS. And voting should be on the weekend.

Create an FDA-Type Commission to Reduce Consumption

Before he died, Erich Fromm wrote a book called *To Have or to Be* in which he grappled with our extreme consumerism. He came up with several very interesting ideas. For instance, he advocated creating a government structure similar to the Food and Drug Administration to encourage what he called "sane consumption." This commission would use a variety of experts such as scientists and sociologists, but would also include theologians, psychologists, and representatives from environmental groups, nonprofits, and social organizations. They would work together to develop a program to reduce consumption and encourage people to consume green products, products that minimize their impact on the earth.

The commission would encourage what is "life-furthering" and discourage what is "life-damaging," developing programs to educate and inspire the public to change. It would think not only in terms of what products and behaviors harm the environment, but what products and behaviors harm people by encouraging passivity, boredom, and destructiveness instead of creativity, participation, and community.

This commission would encourage a strong consumer movement that would use the threat of "consumer strikes" as a weapon.

In Sweden, a similar program has been developed. It's called the Natural Step. A prominent scientist worked with other scientists to agree on a program of sustainability, and the entire country, including the government, schools, businesses, and churches, is active in educating people to live sustainably. There is a growing Natural Step program in this country.

Expand National Service Programs

Related to this could be an expanded national service program, a chance for people to work on solutions to our problems. Jobs would be low paying, but with good benefits, including housing, health care, and educational opportunities. It would be an expanded version of Vista and the Peace Corps, and it could work at educating people about how to live sustainably, helping people to learn to garden organically or develop plans to use fewer household resources.

Continue Efforts toward Establishing Justice

Although we need new policies, we can't neglect what we have started in this century in trying to bring equity and justice to groups without power like women, people of color, old people, people with handicaps, and gays and lesbians. We must continue to support affirmative action and laws that prevent discrimination.

Transform the Global Economy

Focusing on our country is not enough, though. We can never again ignore the global aspects of change. If we make changes in our country, the corporations will move to another country. As we continue to accept the poverty of the rest of the world, we are laying a foundation for future disaster—either through mass starvation and sickness or war. Organizations such as the World Bank must support projects that benefit the poor people of the world without devastating the environment.

ATTACKING THE GIANTS

It wouldn't be easy to bring about these changes. You need a mass social movement with people demanding change. There are two things that stand in the way of such a movement: advertising and corporations. Many feel that we cannot reduce consumption unless we put restraints on corporations and the kind and amount of advertising they do.

Reducing Consumption by Limiting Advertising

In making an argument for the reduction of advertising, we must realize that there are more costs to advertising than meet the eye:

- We pay for advertising in higher prices: $150 billion, or almost $600 per person. Ten percent or more of the price of goods is for promotional costs.

- We lose taxes because advertising costs are considered tax-deductible business expenses. Some estimate that the federal government loses up to $35 billion a year.

- Makers of cigarettes and alcoholic beverages spend $5 billion a year on their advertising, while cigarettes and alcohol kill over

500,000 people each year. Drinking causes traffic fatalities and plays a direct role in violence, particularly domestic violence.

- Advertising supports violence on television, with hundreds of studies linking television violence to violence in real life.

- Advertising undermines parental control as it is increasingly directed toward kids. Schools are one of the latest territories to be invaded by commercialism. Companies give schools brochures, videos about their products, and offer a free news channel, complete with lots of free commercials. Even many of our nonprofit and civic organizations are becoming dependent on corporate funding, making them more likely to be censored in their activities.

- Freedom of the press is undermined. The press is not free to say what it wants for fear of advertising being withdrawn. Advertisers threaten to pull out their money when there are stories and programs that they don't like. Or, they require that a story be written that complements their product. For instance, women's magazines that run ads for cosmetics are often required to run stories about the joys of cosmetic makeovers.

- With the takeover of news networks by entertainment corporations such as Disney, the news gets watered down or programs censored. Almost 90 percent of newspaper editors said, in a 1992 Marquette University study, that advertisers had tried to influence story content, and 37 percent said the newspapers had complied. In another study, half of the business editors surveyed said that advertising pressure had influenced their editorials. Some argue that advertisers' control of the media is a threat to the First Amendment. It is not government controls that are so much the problem, as our founding fathers feared; rather it is something they didn't even dream of: corporate power.

- Our right to privacy is being undermined. Not only is our privacy invaded by the telemarketers' annoying calls at dinner, marketers have volumes of information on all of us. The strange thing is that we often give it freely, in exchange for something "free." For instance, people said that they would fill out survey forms if they were given free movies on television.

In their book, *Marketing Madness,* Michael Jacobson and Laurie Mazur recommend several steps we could take:

- Tax advertising and use the money for consumer information programs such as anti-smoking campaigns.

- Stop advertising aimed at children. (Several European countries have banned TV and radio advertising directed at children.)

- Expand restrictions on alcohol and tobacco advertising. (Canada has banned all cigarette advertising in all media.)

- Restrict telemarketing and direct mail. (Great Britain forbids companies to rent or exchange customer lists unless the customer is told prior to purchasing a product.)

- Expand restrictions on billboards. (This could be done on highways financed with federal funds.)

- Reduce the volume of advertising. (Make it more expensive by raising taxes on it, set time limits on the airwaves, and revitalize the Federal Trade Commission so that it could do its job.)

- Expand Public Broadcasting. (Compared to the United States, Japan spends eighteen times as much per person, Canada spends thirty-two times as much, and Great Britain thirty-eight times as much. Ralph Nader has called for laws that would require all stations to give an hour of prime time daily to community groups.)

Of course, corporations would fight all of this, first by claiming that any curbs would inhibit freedom of speech. But we have always limited speech whenever the damages outweigh the benefits, and in this case, the damage done through the promotion of a consumerist lifestyle is one of the greatest, and most threatening, we have ever faced.

But if we are going to touch advertising, we are going to have to find a way to regulate and reform corporations.

Regulate Corporations

Corporations bring together all the elements of greed that I described earlier. They are run by hierarchy and competition and their goal is to get you to consume by manipulating you with advertising. They are devoted to greed. There is no shilly-shallying—it is only the bottom line that concerns them. This is the primary institution responsible for people's despair, for the destruction of the planet. Yet we go gaily to the shopping centers, keeping corporations in fine fettle, unaware of the affect of corporations on our lives.

Jerry Mander, in his book, *In the Absence of the Sacred,* portrays the way corporations have reached into all corners of our lives:

- With the exception of the government, corporations are the largest landowners in the United States. They are the major financial backers of electoral campaigns, and the major lobbyists for laws that benefit corporate goals.

- If you switch on your radio or television, or open your newspaper, you hear the voice of the corporation in the form of public relations and advertising.

  The basic rule of corporate operation is that it must produce income and show a profit over time. Among publicly held companies there is another basic rule: it must make a *lot* of money. Nothing else counts—the welfare of people and the planet are nothing.

Finally, though, people are beginning to feel that corporate domination isn't fair. Some people fight back by attending shareholder meetings to try to influence corporate policies, but persistent critics of corporate policy have often been faced with legal action. Schor proposes a Corporate Democracy Act that would require corporations to have boards filled with representatives of various stakeholder groups as well as stockholders. In other words, the boards of directors would have to represent the interests of people in general instead of just people who make money from the company.

Ensure Public Participation

To bring about policy changes, we need public participation. We must find ways to help people band together to work for change. We need simplicity circles. We need to support unions and democratically controlled enterprises such as consumer cooperatives, employee-owned firms, and community-owned businesses.

18

TRANSFORMING WORK

If people are highly successful in their professions they lose their sense. Sight goes. They have no time to look at pictures. Sound goes. They have no time to listen to music. Speech goes. They have no time for conversation. Humanity goes. Money making becomes so important that they must work by night as well as by day. Health goes. And so competitive do they become that they will not share their work with others though they have more than they can do themselves. What then remains of a human being who has lost sight, sound, and sense of proportion? Only a cripple in a cave.

—Virginia Woolf

As we work to transform society, we must make changes in the institution that affects us day after day—the workplace. Here is where we can begin to build a movement for change, because here is where people gather together daily.

STATE OF THE WORKPLACE

All of the problems we have looked at emerge in the workplace. Much of our "sleeping sickness of the soul" is caused by conditions in the workplace: long hours, hostile conditions, lack of meaning, anxiety about losing a job.

In the United States, between 50 and 70 percent of people find their jobs so stressful that their health has been affected and their productivity lowered. Job stress brings absenteeism, turnover, lower production, accidents, and rising health insurance. Stress leads to health problems, addictions, and violence against coworkers and family.

WORKPLACE SOLUTIONS

There are two main problems to deal with: we need to help people who have been laid off and also help people who remain employed. Even though more and more people are being laid off, there are many more who remain in the paid workforce, often in low-paying, low-skilled jobs that work them long hours. We need to reform the workplace.

Ultimately, we must push for flexible working hours, shorter working hours, a flattened hierarchy, smaller, decentralized work groups, and increased worker participation in decisions. We must raise low wages and limit extremely high wages. Management must find ways to reduce competitiveness and fear, find ways to share profits, create alternative work schedules, give employees more time and opportunity for learning new skills, and do whatever it can to reduce layoffs.

Some of these solutions could be developed by enlightened management, but many of them will have to come from workers finding ways to pressure employers to change.

This means finding ways to bring people together so that they will begin talking and acting collectively to reclaim some of their power. It means supporting unions, joining professional organizations, and starting study circles. Some nations such as Sweden and Norway now have national legislation requiring employees to give workers some decision-making power in shaping their jobs and workplace environments.

CREATING NEW SOURCES OF INCOME

Anyone who relies totally on the weekly paycheck is foolish, so it's wise to begin to think about alternative sources of income. What are some alternative sources of income we can develop?

Multiple Kinds of Work

Increasingly, people are being more creative about the ways they bring in money. More and more people have two or three sources of income: perhaps a part-time job that brings in a steady source of money and one or two freelance projects. This sounds scary because people find themselves without the usual package of benefits for health or retirement. But these people find ways of coping just as artists have always found ways to survive. Often people purchase private health insurance with a very large deductible, amounting to as high as $5,000. Many of these people use natural and less expensive ways of healing, but they know that if they were in a major accident, they would find some way of paying off the deductible. As for retirement, most of these people do not plan to retire, but just keep working, doing what they love. As more people lose the conventional job package with benefits, government and society will be forced to come up with new solutions. Increasingly, college-educated young people can only find jobs without benefits, and they and their parents will carry more political clout than the traditional poor have.

So how do these people decide what to do? Here's where the idea of earning just $10 for what you love to do can come in. By starting small, you are often able to generate some income, and inspire yourself to continue. We all know about things like catering parties, house cleaning, and delivering pizza—those have become big businesses. But there are also people making money by caring for people's house plants, trimming people's trees, helping people clear out clutter, and running people's errands. One woman even made money getting rid of head lice in kids' hair.

Others teach classes about something they particularly love to do: the person who always loved to dance teaches a dance class; the person who loves to make jewelry teaches jewelry making; the person who loves to take pictures teaches photography. You can teach at continuing education centers in colleges and universities or at churches and neighborhood centers. Teaching classes and workshops can lead to individual or work consultation:

- People don't just consult for corporations, they offer their services to the public. One man who loves sailing not only gives classes on sailing, but consults with people about buying a boat and takes people on outings.

- A man who loved to travel started offering tours through local community colleges and went on to write a book about traveling cheaply. Then he designed and sold his own equipment.

- A woman who goes to thrift stores writes a guide to her local area and begins helping people give garage sales in return for a percentage of the profit.

All of these ways of earning grew out of things people enjoyed doing. The important thing is to be creative in thinking about how you can match up what you love with what others need.

Your Home as a Source of Income

Others have increased their income by renting out a room in their house or selling their house and living communally. The market for this keeps growing as young couples continue to have difficulty buying a house.

In a way, we are returning to our historical roots when families ran boarding houses and people made money any way they could.

Community-Based Businesses

But individual changes are not enough. We also need to rethink how we organize business to guarantee more participant involvement. In her book, *Whole-Life Economics,* Barbara Brandt gives an overview of community-based and community-inspired efforts such as consumer co-ops and locally owned businesses.

Community-Based Money

Communities are developing community-based money systems that let people keep money in a local community and allow all members of the community to be able to afford things, whether they have conventional money or not. Community money systems can take several forms.

Many involve bartering. Some consist of informal bartering systems that individuals set up themselves, in which people exchange services like baby-sitting or plant care. This can be formalized with record-keeping, so the exchanges don't need to be direct. For instance, in our neighborhood, a bartering system gives you points for each hour you put in. Everyone's time is valued equally, and the emphasis is on helping people to learn things, not just doing things for them. If you needed a new fence, you would work alongside the person who knows how to put in a fence, rather than let him or her just do it for you. The overall goal is not just saving people money, but encouraging the development of community.

A more formal arrangement is the LETS system: Local Exchange Trading System, or Local Employment and Trading System. People exchange goods and services for Green Dollars, which are tracked by computer. One of the most complex and successful systems is Ithaca Money, developed in Ithaca, New York. The program prints an "Ithaca HOURS" currency and publishes a newsletter listing bartering options. It's a labor-based currency and each hour is worth $10 and can be used in local businesses for partial payment.

Many of the purchases with HOURS could not have been made with dollars, which the poor spend on necessities. Ithaca HOURS can be used for things like piano lessons or organic foods. The currency for HOURS is even harder to counterfeit than treasury bills.

Community money systems not only help people save money, they build a sense of self-worth. People realize that they can do something that other people value. Above all, these systems build community because people simply interact more.

Worker-Owned Businesses

Many companies are realizing that they will have a hard time surviving unless their workers have a sense of control and ownership. In fact, these companies seem to be more successful than their competitors. Worker-owned firms are about 20 percent more productive than conventional businesses. The ones that do best are the ones that give employees not only stock but a decision-making role.

Socially Responsible Businesses

More and more, people are developing businesses with another goal in mind besides making money, the goal of contributing to the common good.

Our problems are everyone's business! Not just the government's. Minister and author of *The Soul of Politics*, Jim Wallis, suggests that all projects and policies should be subjected to three criteria: Does it expand justice to those at the bottom? Does it allow us to live in harmony with the earth? Does it increase the participation of all people in decision making?

PERSONAL CHANGE

All of these new ways to work are exciting, but what about people who have no hope of enlightened employer practices? Here are some comments of simplicity circle members:

I think about work all the time. I wake up at three in the morning thinking about it and I can't go back to sleep.

I quit because I just got tired of working so hard so that my boss could afford to have three homes.

I quit because of the beating my ego took. I just got tired of not being valued, of being forced to do things that I didn't want to do.

Right now my company is facing a merger, and it has made all of our lives uncertain. You don't know if they will keep you or if they will switch you around. We waste so much time at work just talking about what might happen.

I just hate to go to work. Everyone is starting to knife everyone else in the back. Our department is merging with another one and the management has let it be known that some people are going to be cut. Nobody knows who it will be. Everyone is trying to edge everyone else out. I just can't stand it anymore. I've got to find something else to do. I don't care if I have to take a cut in pay, I've got to find a change.

THINGS TO DO

If you identify with these comments, what can you do? First you should start thinking about getting out in the long-term—start thinking in terms of developing something you love to do, start living frugally, and start educating yourself about new ways to work.

Most important, start getting involved with activities and organizations outside of work. Be open to new ideas and new ways of doing things. Talk to everyone about what they are doing. Gather a group of friends who want to make changes. Several years ago a group of us gathered at a local restaurant once a week in the morning before work and just talked. Having someone listening made a tremendous difference. Out of a group of five people, all of us made significant changes.

People are making changes. It can be done.

The greatest ideas come from reading and talking to others. A large part of simplicity circles is people pooling their knowledge about options they know about and then brainstorming together. Here is an amalgamation of things that people have talked about doing in the simplicity circles.

Create Your Own Niche

Earn money from your passion. One woman saved some money, then quit a large corporation while still unsure about what she was going to do. She loved drama and volunteered to work with a small theater group, helping them get things organized. They discovered that they couldn't get along without her, and hired her. She didn't get nearly as much pay, but she loved what she was doing.

But you don't necessarily have to quit your job to do this. A lot of people find a way of incorporating what they love to do in their work. This entails doing something extra, which can be hard, given how much people are already working. When I was an administrator, I always gave workshops and talks in the community. So when I resigned, I had a ready-made source of income. I not only kept teaching at my school, I taught at many others.

The first thing to do in your present job is to keep focusing on what you like to do, trying to incorporate it in your present work or laying the groundwork for a future career.

Build Community

But focusing on your career is never enough. Work is just no fun if you can't enjoy the people. Once again, our pace of work makes it hard to spend time talking with people, but it is absolutely essential. If you are free to walk around, don't forget to do it. Get to know people on a personal level, and you will come to care for them and they will care for you. Talk to them about their kids and about their hobbies and interests. Work to create community. Organize walking groups, celebrate birthdays, set up simplicity circles. Start a singing group! Go ahead and be outrageous.

And make sure you laugh. I don't know why we think people aren't working hard if they're laughing. Anything that brings people together and helps them feel valued is good. If you are in a supervisory position, schedule times for people to just get together and have coffee and talk. Some build community at work by setting up opportunities for service, such as organizing volunteers to work with groups like Habitat for Humanity or to fix lunches for a homeless shelter. Not only do people feel a sense of accomplishment, they become more caring toward each other.

Reduce Your Work Week

We don't have to wait for a government policy to begin to reduce our work week. We can negotiate to do it ourselves. Start small. Instead of accepting a raise, one woman asked for an extra week of vacation instead. Another woman took a 10 percent reduction in her pay so that she could take off one afternoon a week to work in her daughter's school.

Get Involved in Activities Outside Work

If it's too hard to make changes at work, organize things away from work. In one health maintenance organization, women physicians organized a yearly conference on women in medicine and met for dinner throughout the rest of the year. Don't wait for someone else to do it. You organize it!

Detach

Above all, detach from your work. Many is the time I would say to myself, I am not my job. In fact, don't try to be perfect at work. If you do, you'll work yourself to death. It's good enough to be "good enough."

Act on Your Values

We can give meaning to our work when we see all of life as a chance to act on our values. Express your true self at work, create community, treat people with caring, develop sustainable practices. As the R.E.M. song says, "Stand in the place where you live."

SMALL CHANGES LEAD TO REFORM

In the last chapter we talked about major reforms that the United States needs. Major reforms only come because thousands and thousands of people have made small changes in their lives. The people who are trying to live more simply and trying to create an eco-centric ethic are living lives of mini-experiments. We are figuring out how people can live differently. We are creating new models of wellness and well-being. Someday, when the world no longer has a choice about whether to change—when things become so bad that we *must* change—societies will learn from the people who have been creating changes all along.

PART 7

KEEPING THE FIRES BURNING

STUDY CIRCLES

A nation can be maintained only if, between the state and the individual, there is interposed a whole series of secondary groups near enough to the individuals to attract them strongly in their sphere of action and drag them, in this way, into the general torrent of civil life.

—EMILE DURKHEIM

To me, there's almost nothing as exciting as a group of people gathered around the kitchen table talking. When I was a kid, when my mother spent a social evening at someone's house, she always took me along, and when it would get late, I would fall asleep in the host's bedroom, next to the pile of coats with the murmur of my mother's friends' voices in my ear. That's what we need to re-create.

Somehow we need to bring back this joy of talking together, taking delight in each other and in new ideas and in changing our lives. It's the only way we can meet our needs—our need to be authentic, creative, involved, and to feel connected to something larger than ourselves. None of these comes unless we have community, and true community does not exist without the intimacy and support found within a small group.

Through the simplicity circle, we can keep the fire burning, the fire we have ignited in our hearts and minds as we simplify our lives.

19

DEFINING STUDY CIRCLES

> Never doubt that a small group of thoughtful,
> committed citizens can change the world. Indeed, it is
> the only thing that ever has.
> —MARGARET MEAD

On that day, several years ago, when I sat in our annual opening day ceremonies, listening to the Native American approach to learning, I decided to begin searching for a new kind of adult learning. It seemed vital to me that more adults be excited about and involved in learning—not only for their own sakes, but for the sake of children and for the future of this country. We're always worrying about K–12 education, trying to find ways to improve students' test scores, reduce the number of dropouts, but things don't get much better. Maybe another approach would work: Why not focus on improving adult education? Not the Stanfords and the Harvards; I mean opportunities for adults to keep on learning informally, without grades or tests, an opportunity to find joy and meaning in education—what we traditionally call lifelong learning. I've always thought that if the adults loved learning and kept going to school all their lives, children would follow suit.

So transforming adult education seemed vitally important to me, and I kept searching for the key to adult learning.

Then, one day, I was sitting at my desk reading an article about something called study circles. I had read about study circles in graduate school, about their popularity in Sweden. But I had never found anyone in this country who was interested in them. Here was an organization in Connecticut called the Study Circles Resource Center.

That day I was particularly fed up with my community college president. In hopes of making big money, he wanted me to start setting up computer courses for corporations. "They should be training their own people," I complained to myself. "We're an educational system, not a training facility. We're supposed to be making people think, and develop their abilities, to help them grapple with some of the issues facing them . . . "

I sat there grumbling to myself, disgusted with the politics of higher education. I decided to call the Study Circles Resource Center.

What I found was a small group of people dedicated to the revitalization of democracy in this country. As I began working with the SCRC, I discovered that there were people all over the country using study circles to create an exciting learning experience for adults. Many, many people were beginning to see how study circles could help them with their goals: churches, unions, civic organizations, even newspapers. People were using circles to discuss all sorts of issues: race, war, education.

And so, that January in 1992, I linked study circles to voluntary simplicity. It was a natural match, something that the 175 people who came that night must have sensed. In study circles there were no lectures that bored you; instead, there was exciting and absorbing conversation. You didn't just talk about ideas, you went out and tried them. You didn't just talk about community, you experienced it.

Clearly, here was a form of learning that was transformative. It didn't offer a degree, it offered a transformed life and perhaps a transformed society. It wasn't something you did to get ahead, you did it because it met real needs. It wasn't another commitment hanging over your head, it was something you looked forward to and enjoyed doing. As one participant said, "It would have taken a train running over me to get me to miss my simplicity circle meeting."

Why are study circles so important to people? They are meeting the unmet needs we have been discussing: the need to find your unique path, the need to feel a part of community, the need to be connected to the universe. In study circles you fulfill the human needs to feel connected—to feel valued, to feel accepted, to be appreciated for your authentic self, to feel that you are free to say what you want without fear of being judged, to talk with people who share your values, to talk about matters of importance and substance, to feel you are learning how to feel fully alive.

Simplicity circles give us connection, community, and democracy. They cost almost nothing. They don't require an advanced degree. Here is a way to revolutionize adult learning, and ultimately the world, for all revolutions emerge through the small group.

BACKGROUND

When we look at the history of study circles, their relevance to our times is obvious, for they emerged in a country and a time besieged by problems.

In the early nineteenth century, Sweden was a poor country, many of whose people emigrated to escape starvation. In an effort to find solutions, representatives from the church, the unions, and the Temperance movement visited the United States. There they discovered the Chautauqua movement, a popular nineteenth-century education movement that included home-based study circles. All over New England, small groups of people met together in their living rooms and educated themselves.

The Swedish delegation was impressed and took the idea back home. They instigated hundreds of study circles, enabling peasants to educate themselves, learn how to deal with their problems, and how to govern themselves. Study circles have been credited with helping create the modern Sweden, and today people refer to Sweden as a "study circle democracy."

But it's not just the role of study circles in Sweden's history that is important. Study circles are a central part of Swedish life today, with a third of Swedish citizens involved at any one time, and two-thirds participating at some time in their lives. Study circles help maintain a vital democracy; studies have found that people who participate in study circles are more likely to vote and be involved in civic activities. The government uses study circles to involve citizens in planning and change. Imagine if we had utilized study circles to plan and create a national health-care system. What a different experience and outcome we would have had. Study circles have been referred to as "education by the people, for the people, and of the people."

As I was reading about study circles, I discovered an even more exciting educational-reform movement in a nearby country, Denmark. The Danes also credit an educational reform—something called folk schools—for their modern democracy. Folk schools emerged, once again, from the midst of poverty and social change. The Denmark of the 1860s had suffered half a century of disasters. Many of the most powerful Danes had left and migrated to Germany, leaving a group of demoralized, uneducated peasants. It was from this downtrodden group of people that one of the world's most enlightened democracies emerged. In the Denmark of today, with its high standard of living, universal literacy, and dedication to the welfare of people and the planet, folk schools still have a prominent position.

Folk schools are residential schools with no degrees, credits, or requirements for admission other than a desire for learning and growth. People attend folk schools for anywhere from a few weeks to a whole year. Each school is different, but all are committed to helping people discover how to be responsible for their own learning, how to live together cooperatively, and how to solve personal and societal problems.

They call them schools for life. Simplicity circles draw from both the Swedish tradition of study circles and the Danish tradition of folk schools.

SIMPLICITY STUDY CIRCLES

The phrase *study circles* is a very simple one, yet people always seem to call them study groups or discussion groups. They don't realize that each word in the phrase is very significant.

Study in Study Circles

The word *study* sounds very common and pedestrian. A dull word. It brings up memories of dull experiences: the times we spent studying for a test—memorizing answers, answers that are totally gone, or buried deep within our brain. A waste of time.

But the word *study* should really be very exciting. I was always attracted to Judaism because of the image of men studying the Torah, searching and probing the sacred words, looking for the meaning of life. It was very exciting to me. It seemed to me that this was really what life is all about. We should always be probing, and questioning, and wondering—*studying* is a basic human need. People need to look for meaning and understanding. They want to answer those basic life questions: Who am I? How shall I live my life? How can I be happy? This is what studying is really all about, but it's rarely the stuff we do in schools.

And then, I discovered the Latin root for the word *study*. I couldn't believe it! It means enthusiasm and zest—the very qualities we are searching for in our quest to be fully alive! This is the true meaning of study.

Circles as Connectedness

And the word *circle* has its own significance. Why is a circle such a profound symbol? A circle stands for life itself. We think of "The Great Circle of Life." The earth is round, the Sun is round. Circles form in the water when we throw in a pebble; the tree trunk is round. The circle is so often the shape of nature. Life moves in cycles from birth to death and rebirth.

The circle is a shape that connects people. We think of people joining hands, people dancing, women sitting in a circle and sewing. And connectedness is one of the most basic needs we have. If we don't feel connected to nature and to one another, we won't survive. We won't learn to work together to bring about change. It is connection that engenders caring, and only caring will save us. The circle is a symbol of equality, of a rejection of dominance and an embracing of equality and partnership. Only if we learn to be equals will our democracy survive. Only if democracy survives will we survive.

RESPONDING TO LIFE

As we come to the close of this century, what will we remember? What emerges for me is our *failure to respond*. We are not responding to the earth as it dies. We did not respond as the Jews were taken away. We did not respond when Kitty Genovese was killed. We do not respond as we walk by the homeless. We don't respond when our wife or husband says "We've got to talk."

We sit passively staring at the television.

How do we revive people, get them to start seeing and hearing and talking and taking action? How do we get people to be involved, engaged, engrossed, absorbed, concerned, dedicated? How do we get them to step forward and commit to life, commit to being fully alive? How do we get people to participate in the life around them?

They can learn to participate by being in a study circle, an experience that does not succeed unless all participate—unless everyone talks, everyone listens, everyone takes action. There is no place for the person who wants to sit back with bemused detachment. Study circles can revive us, keeping the fire burning in our souls.

20

WHY STUDY CIRCLES?

As long as you live, keep learning how to live.
—SENECA

Let us then discuss as quickly as we can the sort of
education that is needed . . . let it be founded on
poverty. . . . Next, what should be taught in the new
college, the poor college? Not the arts of dominating
other people; not the arts of ruling, of killing, of
acquiring land and capital. . . . It should teach the arts
of human intercourse; the art of understanding other
people's lives and minds, and the little arts of talk.
. . . The aim of the new college, the cheap college,
should be not to segregate and specialize, but to
combine. It should explore the ways in which mind and
body can be made to cooperate; discover what new
combinations make good wholes in human life. The
teachers should be drawn from the good livers as well
as from the good thinkers. . . . Competition would be
abolished. Life would be open and easy. People who
love learning for itself would gladly come there.
Musicians, painters, writers, would teach there,
because they would learn. What could be of greater
help to a writer than to discuss the art of writing with
people who were thinking not of examinations or
degrees or of what honour or profit they could make
literature give them but of the art itself?
. . . They would come to the poor college and practise
their arts there because it would be a place where
society was free; not parcelled out into the miserable
distinctions of rich and poor, of clever and stupid; but
where all the different degrees and kinds of mind, body

and soul merit operated. Let us then found this new
college; this poor college; in which learning is sought
for itself; where advertisement is abolished; and there
are no degrees; and lectures are not given, and sermons
are not preached, and the old poisoned vanities and
parades which breed competition and jealousy. . . . The
letter broke off there.

—VIRGINIA WOOLF

Virginia Woolf wrote *Three Guineas,* from which the quotation
above is taken, on the eve of World War II, shortly before she ended
her life by walking into the sea. In this passage, Woolf is answering
a letter to someone who has asked her to use her influence to help
stop war. In considering how to stop war, she naturally thinks of
education, but she realizes that education helps produce war,
because it perpetuates the traditions of competition and greed. So
she proposes a free college, an experimental college.

That's what simplicity study circles are: they are free schools,
schools for life, a learning experience that helps people break free.
Their goal is similar to Woolf's goal: to teach people to talk together
about real things and make real changes.

In one sense, study circles are remedial. They are trying to correct or counteract the evils and failures of our schooling. Virginia
Woolf captures the true meaning of what study circles do—teach us
the *arts of human intercourse* and how to be *good livers* as well as *good
thinkers.* This is not what we learn in school.

Think about your experience in school. What was it like? Do
humiliation and shame come to mind? One woman remembered a
time in her childhood when she was singing with the other kids, and
the teacher stopped and said, "So you're the one who's been singing
flat!" She never sang in school again.

Most of us have a story like that. My worst one was from graduate school, when I would meet with my dissertation committee. As
I sat there listening to them tear my work to shreds, I kept repeating
to myself, "I am not going to cry." Since that time, I've always

thought about writing an article called "Groveling My Way to a Doctorate." It's hard to get through school with your sense of self-esteem in good shape.

But it's not just that schools undermine our self-esteem, they seem to be totally unaware that there are problems in the world. Schools act as if there is nothing wrong. They act like the environment has nothing to do with them. But our problems are everyone's problems.

To more fully understand the need for study circles, we need to get a clearer picture of how schools are failing us.

HOW SCHOOLS FAIL US

- Schools are not giving people the skills to solve the problems they will face in life. In fact, many of our problems in the world are caused by educated people. It was educated people who developed the nuclear bomb, educated people who develop weapons; it is educated people who use up the world's resources.

- Our schools fail to nurture the values of *caring and community*—values that people will increasingly need to survive in an ugly world. Instead, we are taught to compete and win. Without a value system of caring, a community will not survive. Many of the Germans working with Hitler were highly educated people.

- Our system of *democracy is undermined* because students don't experience democracy in the classroom. Democracy doesn't just mean voting. It means participating, joining in, speaking up, having your say, getting involved. Instead, students sit and take notes and ask, "Will that be on the test?"

- We live in a society where most people have *inferiority* complexes. When you're working for a grade, you're working on someone else's goals and learning someone else's answers—and you're not developing the inner authority that allows you to believe in yourself.

- Schools also give us *superiority* complexes. Schools encourage an arrogance in us, causing us to disregard the ideas of other cultures at home and around the world.

- By focusing on the intellect and learning to be "objective," *we do not learn to feel deeply about things* and thus, cannot discover our passion, or care about the problems facing us, or even develop lasting relationships. If you ever got really excited about something in college, you knew that you had lost the argument. To win, you had to stay cool.

- We learn an *adversarial approach to the truth*. We learn to fight over who's right or wrong, who possesses the truth. It's a consumerist approach to the truth. We learn that truth is something that exists independently of us. It's something the people who write books know, something that only the "great minds" possess. We don't learn that there are many different routes to the truth, that we can all create and discover knowledge and wisdom ourselves.

- The academic world makes us feel inferior about our intelligence because the academic world *speaks in jargon which few can understand*. People feel stupid when they read an academic work. They don't say, "Why can't this person communicate better!" They say, "I can't understand, I must be stupid."

Education as it exists *creates a caste system*. In our society people with more education not only get better jobs, they are treated with more deference, have more privileges. Schools are often only a "legitimizing factor," that is, it is really one's income and educational background that guarantee success. Of course, a few poor people always sneak through so that people can say the system is fair. Tokens are always used to make a closed system seem open. Schools support a society that is "parcelled out into the miserable distinctions of rich and poor, of clever and stupid."

We need something different. We need to develop, again in Virginia Woolf's words, "good livers as well as good thinkers." Nell Noddings, Stanford professor of education and author of *Caring*, says the main role of schools should be *caring*—to teach caring and to give students the experience of being cared for. Imagine if we adopted Nodding's curriculum: caring for the self, caring for others, caring for the planet, caring for animals, caring for things. One simple concept and we could change the world.

Ultimately, schools should move away from their narrow focus on training people for jobs. They must focus on *learning for life*: learning that is concerned about the preservation of life, learning that helps people live life fully.

SIMPLICITY CIRCLES AS LEARNING FOR LIFE

Life-Enhancing

Learning for life is the central concept of simplicity circles. In *learning for life* simplicity circles, the purpose is to learn how to live life to the fullest. You don't struggle to memorize a computer program that may be out of date when you get a job. You learn how to discover what really gives you joy. In this approach to education, you don't just read and take notes on a book and continue with life as usual—you renew and revitalize your life.

Life-Transforming

Did your schools really transform your life? Can you even remember one fraction of the facts you learned? All those facts we memorized! What difference did it make? *Learning for life* is not about gaining credentials or absorbing information. Simplicity circles help you become a different person, a transformed person.

Learning to Sustain Life

In school, we learn a little about our ancestors, but do we ever discuss our descendants? That is, do we think about what life will be like for our grandchildren, do we learn to care about them? Simplicity circles must help us discover how to live so that future generations can live.

Answering Basic Life Questions

When was Napoleon born? What is the theory of relativity? Would you rather learn to answer those questions or the basic life questions of Who am I? and How should I live my life? Which set of questions will help you live more fully? Simplicity circles help you discover the meaning and purpose of life.

Whole-Life Learning

Think of a person you admire. Are they cold and rational, inspiring respect and fear? Or are they warm and lively, people who smile and laugh a lot? Can you connect with them emotionally as well as intellectually? No one learns with just their head. We need to integrate emotional, intellectual, spiritual, and moral learning. In Woolf's words, "The aim of the new college . . . should be not to segregate and specialize, but to combine. It should explore the ways in which mind and body can be made to cooperate; discover what new combinations make good wholes in human life." Simplicity circles combine laughter with reflection, feeling with analysis.

Living Democracy

What is one of the most humiliating thing you can experience? To be raked over the coals by your boss, to be chastised and demeaned and not be able to respond, not speak up and defend yourself. That is the workplace for many today. Our life blood is speaking up. Defending our own dignity: that's the core of democracy. Simplicity circles strive for a democratic community—a community based on the belief in the individual, a belief that the common person must be treated with dignity. It is the belief that the average citizen must speak up, be listened to, and make a difference. It is the belief that experts and authorities won't solve our problems, only the ordinary person has this power.

In a simplicity circle, since people are equal and equally responsible, they learn to move away from domination and submission. A simplicity circle creates what Lappe and Dubois call *living democracy*—democracy that gives power to the ordinary citizen.

Understanding Life Around Us

How do you decide how to vote? How do you decide what car to buy? People need to be able to make decisions in their own long-term best interests and to recognize when others, like politicians or advertisers, are trying to manipulate or exploit them. In simplicity circles people share their knowledge, pool their information, help each other analyze the forces in everyday life that work to undermine the common good.

Enlivenment: Bringing New Vitality to Learning and Life

How many lectures did you fall asleep in during college? How often did you drag from class to class, waiting for the day to be over to begin your real life? Or, think about the way you would freeze up around some college professors. I remember an economics teacher I had in graduate school. There was no way I would risk raising my hand and suffering one of his cutting comments. My mind was numbed by dread of his sarcastic statements. Students often find themselves bored and dozing in one class, scared to death in another. How much learning takes place?

Learning shouldn't be boring or deadening or full of fear.

Learning should make us feel alive, excited about life: it should be *enlivening*. Simplicity circles are enlivening because people are talking about real things and no one is grading you or judging you. People leave each meeting feeling more energetic, more hopeful—more alive.

Simplicity circles, then, are vital to preserving life, to understanding life, and to living life fully. They are a way to make life "open and easy. People who love learning for itself would gladly come there."

21

THE HOW OF STUDY CIRCLES

Why should we leave it to Harper & Brothers and
Redding & Co. to select our reading?
                    —HENRY DAVID THOREAU

Real education begins with a question in the life of the
learner.
                    —LEO TOLSTOY

We have stories to tell, stories that provide wisdom
about the journey of life. What more have we to give
one another than our "truth" about our human
adventure as honestly and as openly as we know how?
                    —RABBI SAUL RUBIN

Listening is a magnetic and strange thing, a creative
force. . . . When we are listened to, it creates us, makes
us unfold and expand. Ideas actually begin to grow
within us and come to life. . . . When we listen to
people there is an alternating current, and this
recharges us so that we never get tired of each other . . .
and it is this little creative fountain inside us that
begins to spring and cast up new thoughts and
unexpected laughter and wisdom. . . . Well, it is when
people really listen to us, with quiet fascinated
attention, that the little fountain begins to work again,
to accelerate in the most surprising way.
                    —BRENDA UELAND

How can we conduct our simplicity circles so that we can experience the "magnetic and creative force" Brenda Ueland talks about?

How can we "unfold and expand," feel recharged, have "ideas actually begin to grow within us and come to life?" That's not our usual experience when discussing ideas with others—more often we end up competing for air time, going home exhausted and sometimes feeling angry. We need to experience discussion as an "alternating current," an experience of "new thoughts and unexpected laughter and wisdom."

How can we do that? How can we learn to really listen to each other? When my son was little he used to take my face in his hands and hold it while he talked. Although grabbing someone's face might indeed be an effective way to get someone to listen, it's not what I am recommending. Instead, I have developed a methodology that helps people to experience conversation in the transformative way that Ueland describes.

I'm sure that in another time, when people spent more time talking with each other, having guidelines on how to converse would have seemed ludicrous. Nonetheless, I've found that today we need them. Otherwise we drift back into our classroom patterns, becoming either like members of a debate team trying to shoot down each other's ideas or like passive students expecting a teacher to take responsibility. The guidelines and format that are described below grow out of my philosophy of *learning for life,* and from many years of teaching and conducting simplicity study circles.

GUIDELINES

No Leaders: Be Participatory

To solve our world's problems, we need people's participation. There are so many books about how to be a good leader, instead, we need books about how to be good followers: that is, about how people can follow without allowing themselves to be led, who can be people full participants. Study circles are the place to learn!

This is a circle, not a pyramid, so there is no leader—everyone is responsible. As one simplicity circle member described it, the circle is leader-full, not leaderless. But with no one running a discussion, groups can deteriorate into a few people dominating the floor. Instead of having a *leader*, I suggest that the circle have a *coordinator*, because the word *leader* is loaded with meanings that run counter to the democratic philosophy of a study circle. Having a *coordinator* suggests that everyone is equally important and involved.

But a lot of people feel nervous about being a coordinator. Following this simplicity circle format will make anyone feel comfortable being the coordinator.

Respond as Equals

People will participate fully only when they respond as equals. When you are in a subordinate position, you distrust your own judgment and learn to sabotage those with more power. When you are in a superior position, you become arrogant and close yourself off to new information. You quit listening and learning and become defensive and hostile if anyone questions you.

But too often we find ourselves jockeying for position, showing deference to those *above* us and ignoring those *below* us. In study circles we *act* on the idea that we are all equals. No one person's opinions are more important than another's. In particular, we don't defer to people with higher degrees: the physician or professor shouldn't be listened to any more carefully than the waitress.

View Conversation as Barn-Raising Instead of Battle

Think of how you felt the last time you were in a discussion. Did you go home relaxed and happy, or did you get into the car and immediately start ranting about the way that bastard Frank carried on, the way he tried to push his ideas on everyone, the way he refused to listen . . .

Discussion in our society is often a battle we must fight to the death—proving that we know more, that we're smarter, that we're just plain right. What most of these guidelines are trying to do is to help us avoid having discussions that end as battles. When conversation is a contest, our sense of self-worth is injured, our relationships with others are damaged, and we rarely learn anything new.

As a result, we tend to avoid conversation about ideas. We stick to talking about restaurants or movies. A Merck Family Fund study confirmed this: it found that people would *like* to talk about our country's materialism and greed, but they are worried about the hostility it would generate.

Michael Kahn, author of the *Tao of Conversation,* explores an approach to discussion that helps us avoid the tendency to turn conversations into contests. Building on the philosophy of Martin Buber, the Jewish theologian, Kahn suggests that we learn to create *I-thou* relationships, relationships in which we accept the other person as they are, not trying to change them into what we want them to be.

In an I-thou conversation our goal is not to win, but to improve our relationships, learn something new, and have everyone leave the conversation feeling good about themselves.

So how do we avoid having conversations become battles? Kahn suggests that we think of the conversation as a "barn-raising." You help the other people build their ideas, and then they can help you build yours. If a better idea emerges, that's great. But essentially, you are trying to help others come up with their own truths.

Kahn recommends keeping in mind certain attitudes that help you remember not to think in terms of "right or wrong" or "agree or disagree":

- Persuasion is not the goal.

- The conversers are each other's teachers and students.

- People need reinforcement, recognition, validation. When an idea is interesting or helpful, it is important to acknowledge that it is.

- Questions are useful parts of conversations, but challenges are not.

This approach works well because research finds that fear and anger inhibit thinking, and when we start arguing, we often feel angry and defensive. When you argue, you're not really accepting the other, because you are trying to change him or her. It's helpful to remember that opinions are only ways of stating our current thoughts. Thoughts should always be in process, and we should always be open, always taking in new information.

Kahn roots his ideas in his reading of Plato, who believed that we all know a lot more than we think and that wisdom is buried in each one of us, needing only a good listener to help it emerge.

So instead of thinking of a conversation as a contest or a battle, think of it as a barn-raising, something that you are all working on together. As others speak, try to suppress the instinct to criticize or compare. In college we learned to listen with a machete in our hand, ready to jump in and shred others' ideas. Let your first response be one of understanding. When your experience is different, or you disagree with someone, a good response is often, "I can see how you might feel that way, given your experience, but this is what happened to me . . ." There is more than one version of truth or reality.

Obviously, there is no attacking, dismissing, or denigrating others' ideas. This should be obvious, but surprisingly, some people still respond to others' ideas with smirks or derogatory laughs. Everyone must feel absolutely safe about speaking up.

No playing devil's advocate. Although this is a common form of communication, it violates just about all of the above guidelines. "Devil's advocate" questions are really statements or criticisms in disguise. When someone says to me, "Let me play devil's advocate for a minute," I always respond with, "I'd rather you didn't."

Be Authentic

We spend a lot of our lives trying to look successful: acting as if our families have no problems, that we love our work, that we know

what we're doing. No one really gets to know us. We join study circles to have relationships of depth, so we must strive to be real, to be
as authentic as possible. So speak with the emotion that you feel.
Don't censor yourself, don't try to sound intelligent, don't try to
sound sophisticated, don't pretend you know something you don't.
Take the risk telling the truth, doing it with kindness and respect.
Once you realize that you aren't in a contest, this authenticity comes
easily.

Discover Wisdom through Stories

Authenticity comes easily because the core of the simplicity
circle is people's stories, people's personal experience. Throughout
most of human history, people learned by telling stories. I've come
to believe that just as people have a need for safety and security, for
companionship and caring, they also have a need to hear stories.
Hearing stories is essential for many reasons:

- Stories show the universality of human experience. We begin to
  see that we all share the same needs. When people feel alone in
  their personal experiences, they can start to think they are crazy.
  Others' stories show them that they are not. People involved in
  simplifying their lives often feel they are swimming upstream
  and need to feel like they are not alone.

- Stories are a safe way to express our feelings. Because feelings
  are excluded from the academic world, most of us are wary
  about expressing our feelings in conversations with others. We
  think we are supposed to sound objective and unbiased.
  Expressing feelings helps us learn to experience that absolutely
  essential emotion—*caring.*

- Stories undermine the elitist nature of our education. Everyone
  can understand a story. Everyone can tell a story. And stories
  are open to all sorts of interpretations. There is no one right
  interpretation. Stories are a move away from the academic lan-

guage of education—language that is expressed in ways that the ordinary person can't understand.

- Ultimately, stories connect people, because no matter how unique you are, someone else has had the same experience.

Question Conventional Wisdom and Seek Alternative Views

Simplicity circles are subversive. Conventional wisdom usually works to maintain the current power imbalance, protect the status quo, slow down change. Remember, increasingly we are getting only a very narrow view of reality—the corporate view. As people begin to read about simplicity, they bring back to the circle new ideas. People learn from each other and begin to challenge what Toni Morrison called the "master narrative": the ultimate story of our nation that tells us to give our power away to others.

CIRCLE ACTIVITIES

There are several important concepts in simplicity circles that distinguish them from other types of discussions: the use of small groups, the role of the coordinator, the use of reflection, the technique of taking turns, the check-in, the action steps, the personal research, and the journal.

Use of Small Groups

The ideal group size is six to eight people. When the group is bigger, intimacy is lost and individuals have less time to talk. I have found it helpful to also use even smaller groups—to talk in pairs or in threes before opening discussion to the larger group. This allows for greater depth than you can have in the larger group. (When the discussion question is more personal, groups of twos work well; when the questions are more analytical, groups of three seem to work better.) Talking in twos or threes before talking in front of the group is like writing a rough draft before doing the final paper: people feel more confident in what they have to say and they come up with even better ideas.

Coordinator Position

The main role of the coordinator is helping the group follow the format—moving people from one section to the next. Since the format is very detailed, the coordinator does not have to worry about being an experienced discussion leader.

It's good if the coordinator position can be rotated.

Reflection

Reflection is an important part of conversation, but in our frenzy-filled days, we neglect it. In the circles, before discussing a question, we take a few minutes to think about the answers. People sit quietly and make notes on their thoughts. When people take just a few minutes to think, the discussions are much better.

Taking Turns

The ordinary method of leading a group discussion is horrible. Almost no one is good at it because it is a flawed method. What usually happens is this: The group leader asks a question. But it isn't really a real question, it's a question designed to manipulate people into talking. People feel they are being manipulated and they just sit there. I remember asking such a question once to a group of high school kids, and one boy responded with, "I hate the Socratic method!" And I realized that he was right, that we are being dishonest when we do that. What we are really saying is "Guess the answer that's in my head."

So in simplicity circles, we ask real questions that people can answer from their own experience. But we don't just throw out a question like we're throwing a bone to a bunch of dogs to wrestle over. That just turns conversations into contests and everyone gets anxious, with the quiet ones resentful because they don't get to speak, and the talkative ones resentful because they aren't getting to speak enough. We have to eliminate the anxiety about speaking up.

I was once in a group where they tried to solve this dilemma by only allowing the quiet ones to speak first, making the rest of us wait. The talkative ones *were* more quiet, and the more reticent members *did* talk more, but something else happened: the conversations often dragged and lacked energy. Having the quiet people begin the conversation meant that a low energy level was established and there wasn't as much zest in the conversation, so this was not a satisfactory solution. Perhaps we need to accept the fact that some people will always talk more and others talk less, and, knowing that, just make sure everyone has a chance to talk.

What I have found works best is that after you discuss a question in small groups of two or three, you again answer the question—this time more succinctly—by taking turns going around the circle. When you proceed around the circle, there is absolutely no competition for air time. Everyone relaxes because everyone knows they will have a chance to speak. They also can relax and listen because they have already considered what they are going to say. They don't have to sit there preparing their answer. They can really concentrate on listening.

To make sure no one talks too long, you can use a timer, giving people only three minutes each to talk. An old-fashioned hourglass-style egg timer is nice because there is no annoying ding, but any kind will do. Now, using this format doesn't mean that people can't be flexible and allow someone to finish their thought when their time is up, but having a timer means the coordinator does not have to be a police officer. To have a good discussion, people must feel totally safe to speak up, so it's important that they don't have to worry about having others trying to quiet them *or* draw them out.

This method of going around the circle and taking turns speaking is similar to the method used in twelve-step groups. People are telling their feelings and thoughts, not trying to convince anyone or come up with the right answer. And what they say doesn't even have to relate to what the others say, although a theme usually emerges. In twelve-step groups "cross talk" is discouraged. This is to dissuade people from giving advice and opinions. In the simplicity circle, conversation will often spontaneously break out when someone responds to what someone else has said. If the outburst of conversation goes on too long, the coordinator reminds people to move on to the next person and continue around the circle. The spontaneous talk that emerges is much richer than the comments a leader tries to pull out of people.

Check-In

Except for the first meeting, you will begin each session with a brief check-in. This involves going quickly around the circle with people reporting on some of the things they did that week: concrete actions they took to simplify their lives. No one should take more than one minute to report, and people should feel free to pass. During the check-in, people talk about ways they have *cut back on something*—the kinds of things discussed in chapters 5 and 6: getting rid of clutter, consuming less, eliminating things in your life that you don't want to do, saying no to claims on your time.

This is always fun and interesting. When people talk about specific things they do, they are always interesting! And people feel a tremendous reinforcement for making further changes—when something goes well for someone, everyone is pleased. Sometimes people talk about things they tried and failed, with the rest of the group helping them figure out what to do differently.

You also get lots of ideas from others about things you can do. People share information on where to get mulch for their garden, simple recipes for dinner parties, their favorite consignment stores, ideas about getting rid of clutter, what the best bus lines are, and on and on.

Actions for the Coming Week

The check-in is a report on the activities people commit to at the end of each session. When people commit to doing something, they are more likely to do it. For instance, if you say that you are going to drive less, you will be more likely to take some action because you know that people will be waiting to hear how you did. So, a few minutes before the end of the session, you whip around the circle with each person talking about an action he or she will take the following week. You decide on something specific you want to cut back on: driving less, spending less money, eating out less, getting rid of your piles of paper. You pick *something*. You may end up doing something else, but this gives you a focus.

Personal Research

Besides experimenting with changing a behavior, each circle member should conduct personal research on issues. This is more than just reading. It is research done in the Native American spirit of watching the beavers, always asking yourself, "What did I see, what did I feel, what did I learn?" This means that we break the habit of having all of our information come from books or the television, that we learn to build our own conclusions from our own experience.

As you will see in the format below, there are three kinds of personal research: thinking, questioning, and observing. You think about the question of the week; you talk casually about issues with acquaintances during the week; and you watch how people behave. You record your observations, thoughts, and feelings in your journal.

Journal

Everyone should have a journal, a notebook, or something to write in that will be used throughout all of the sessions. They will be used during the circle meetings to write your thoughts and notes in, and they will be used during the week to record thoughts and observations. Some people will write in them a lot, and some very little. It just depends on your temperament. I have found that it is impossible to require people to write in their journals every night, because only a few follow through.

LOGISTICS

Organizing a Simplicity Circle

There are lots of places to organize a study circle: in a community college, a neighborhood center, at church, at work, or in your neighborhood. Get a core group of two or three people and find a way to publicize it. Talk to the people who run community-education programs in your local community college or neighborhood center about having a simplicity circle as part of their program.

Meeting Places

In Seattle most study circles meet in people's homes. They could be anywhere, but people like the intimacy and informality that a home brings. We try to organize them by neighborhood so that nobody has to drive very far.

Meeting Times

A study circle should last for at least ten weeks. Many in Seattle have continued for years, but for a new group, there should be a definite beginning and ending date. At the end of that period, the people can decide on their next step.

In the beginning it is important to meet once a week so that a solid group forms. Two hours is a good length. The person whose house it is in can decide if the group will meet from 7:00 to 9:00 or 7:30 to 9:30. Some hold morning groups.

Sharing of Books

It's good if everyone has a copy of *Circle of Simplicity* (of course I would say that!), but that shouldn't be a requirement to join a circle. Try to make arrangements to share books. Maybe among a circle of six to eight people there could be three or four books. People who live close to each other could share a book. It's important that the person who will be coordinating the meeting will have been able to read the corresponding chapters in the book.

Flexibility

Since a simplicity study circle is meant to be democratic, ultimately people can decide for themselves what they want to do. However, I have found simplicity circles to be more successful if people start out by using the format outlined below.

Also, it's good to be a little flexible about the starting time. People should try to be on time, but not rush—rushing undermines everything we're trying to do. It's good to have a social period at the beginning, anyway. Simplicity circles are meant to be enjoyable. I think it's nice to have refreshments, but the group can decide if they are too much of a bother. One of our longest running circles feels strongly that refreshments are a hassle! Try to start the discussion no later than fifteen to twenty minutes after the designated starting time.

Even though I recommend being flexible with the beginning time, it's important to end on time. Doing otherwise may be too hard on the host.

Format

Note: As you proceed through the ten weeks, there will be fewer and fewer details in the instructions, because the group will be more skilled in discussion.

Session One: Introductions

Purpose: The first night will be different from subsequent meetings, because the focus the first night is getting to know each other.

Preparation (The preparations should be done during the week preceding the discussion.): For the first meeting, participants should have read part 1, "The Awakening of Soul," and part 2, "Getting Clear."

Opening: The first night the coordinator gives some background about why he or she organized the circle. People will introduce themselves when they talk in the circle. Name tags are helpful.

1: Reflection: Begin by reflecting for a few minutes on these questions and jotting answers in your journal:

- Why are you here? What is going on in your life that attracts you to the subject of voluntary simplicity?

- How do you define voluntary simplicity?

- What are you already doing to simplify your life?

2: Small group discussion: In pairs, discuss the answers to your questions, taking 5 to 10 minutes, dividing the time between each of you.

3: Large group discussion: Go around the circle and summarize what you said in your pairs. Just answer for yourself. This will take up most of the first evening, so divide up the time accordingly.

4: Action commitments: Go around the circle and decide on one thing you will cut back on: clutter, time commitments, people you spend time with.

5: End the first session by discussing logistics questions:

- Have people give addresses and phone numbers so that everyone can write them down in their journals.

- Set up a buddy system. If one of you misses, the other can catch you up on what happened.

- See if people can arrange car pools.

- Discuss the issue of refreshments.

Session Two: Understanding Study Circles

Purpose: The purpose of this session is to continue to talk about ways to cut back on your activities and to discuss the philosophy of the study circle method of learning.

Preparation: Read part 2, "Getting Clear," and part 7, "Keeping the Fires Burning."

Personal research: Question for the week: What negative educational experiences have you had?

Think: Recall negative learning experiences you have had in your life.

Question: In your conversations with acquaintances during the week, ask people about negative experiences they have had in education.

Observe: Observe people in discussion, and figure out what makes the discussions effective or ineffective.

1: Check-in. Report on last week's action commitments.

2: Reflection: Think of a negative learning experience you had in school. Sit quietly for a few minutes and jot down things that you remember.

3: Small group discussion: Divide into pairs and discuss your answers.

4: Large group discussion: Go around the circle giving a capsule summary of your story and relating it to what you know about the philosophy of simplicity circles. Discuss how your experience would have been different if schools were conducted with the principles of simplicity circles. For instance, many people will remember their fear of speaking up in class—something that would not happen with a simplicity circle philosophy that turns discussion battles into "barn-raising" conversations.

5: Comments: Report on things learned that week in the process of personal research. No need to go around the circle. Anyone who wants can contribute.

6: Action commitments: Go quickly around the circle with each person committing to cutting back on something the next week.

Session Three: Transforming Personal Consumption

Purpose: The purpose of this session is to understand why we need to reduce consumption, why we consume, and how we can reduce consumption.

Preparation: Read chapter 6, "Getting Clear: Transforming Consumption."

Personal research: Question for the week: What is something you bought that you regret buying? Why did you buy it?

Think: Consider the question: Why do Americans consume so much?

Question: Ask people about things they have regretted buying and why they bought them.

Observe: Observe what people buy in stores. Ask yourself "What did I see; what did I feel; what did I learn?"

1: Check-in: Report on ways you reduced your consumption during the week.

2: Reflection: Think about something you bought that you regret buying.

3: Small group discussion: Talk in groups of three about your experiences and discuss why Americans consume so much.

4: Large group discussion: Go around the circle and summarize your experience, linking your experience to the question of why Americans consume so much.

5: Comments: Report on personal research.

6: Action commitments: Coordinator leads the group in brainstorming ways to reduce consumption. Go around the circle, telling what activity you are going to focus on this week.

Session Four: Finding Your Passion

Purpose: To discover your personal gift—the thing you love to do.

Preparation: Read part 3, "Trail Seekers."

Personal research: Question for the week: What is something you love to do?

Think: Is there something in your life that is a constant theme, something you have always loved to do?

Question: Ask people who seem to enjoy their work how they discovered what they liked to do.

Observe: Watch people's faces and see how often they are smiling and laughing.

1: Check-in. Report on activities.

2: Reflection: Think of something you love to do and why you don't do more of it.

3: Small group discussion: Discuss in pairs.

4: Large group discussion: Go around the circle with each person talking about what they love to do and why they don't do more of it.

5: Comments: Report on personal research.

6: Action commitments: Go around the circle, telling what you are going to do that will bring you more pleasure.

Session Five: Passion, Continued

Purpose: To think of ways you can earn money from your passion.

Preparation: Review part 3, "Trail Seekers."

Personal research: Question for the week: Think of something you love to do that someone would pay you $10 for.

Think: What are ways you have already earned money doing what you love to do? What can you learn from those examples?

Question: Ask people for ideas on how you could earn money doing what you love.

Observe: Watch for stories in magazines and the paper on people who have started unusual businesses.

1: Check-in: Usual.

2: Reflection: Reflect on question for the week.

3: Small group discussion: Talk in groups of three about the question.

4: Large group discussion: Go around the circle, with the group brainstorming each person's idea, trying to think of different ways they can earn money from something they love to do.

5: Comments: Report on personal research.

6: Action commitments: Usual.

Session Six: Building Community

Purpose: To learn how to build more community in our lives.

Preparation: Read part 4, "Wood Gatherers."

Personal research: Question of the week: Think of a time in your life when you experienced community.

Think: What were the central elements that made it into community?

Question: Ask people about times they experienced community.

Observe: Watch for examples of community in your neighborhood.

1: Check-in: Usual.

2: Reflect: Reflect on the question for the week.

3: Small group discussion: Discuss the question for the week in pairs.

4: Large group discussion: Go around the circle and summarize your experiences, listing the factors in your experience that you think defined community.

5: Comments: Coordinator leads brainstorming on ways people can develop community.

6: Action commitments: Go around the circle with each person saying one thing they want to do to create community in their lives.

Session Seven: Community, Continued

Purpose: To understand how society discourages community and to think of ways to encourage community at work.

Preparation: Review part 4, "Wood Gatherers," and read part 6, "Torch Bearers."

Personal research: Question of the week: What in our society discourages community? How could we encourage community at work?

Think: When have you experienced community at work?

Question: Ask others about how people could have more community at work.

Observe: Watch for stories in the newspaper about community activities going on in your city.

1: Check-in: Discuss your efforts to build community.

2: Reflection: Reflect on question of the week.

3: Small group discussion: Discuss question of the week in groups of three.

4: Large group discussion: Go around the circle with each person addressing two issues: the things in our society that undermine community and what they could do at work to create community.

5: Comments: Report on personal research.

6: Action commitments: Focus on building community.

Session Eight: Living Mindfully

Purpose: To understand how to slow down and live mindfully.
Preparation: Read part 5, "Fire Makers."
Personal research: Question of the week: Think about ways you could slow down and live mindfully, particularly ways you can become more involved with nature. (Since it is hard to discuss the subject of spirituality, this can be saved for some time in the future for people who continue on together and know each other better.)

Think: What are some of the negative consequences of rushing? Think of times when you were rushing and everything fell apart.

Question: Ask people some of the foolish things they have seen people do when they were rushing. For instance, things people do in their cars.

Observe: Watch for examples of people rushing—people being rude, people being impatient.

1: Check-in: What are things you have done to build community?

2: Reflection: Think of areas in which you would like to be able to slow down.

3: Small group discussion: Discuss in pairs ways you want to slow down, and techniques that have helped you slow down.

4: Large group discussion: Discuss techniques that help you slow down.

5: Comments: Coordinator leads brainstorming and makes a list of elements of additional things we can do to slow down.

6: Action commitments: Have each person tell how they will try to slow down.

Session Nine: Transforming Work

Purpose: To think of ways you can improve your work situation.

Preparation: Review chapter 18, "Transforming Work."

Personal research: Question of the week: What are some of the ways you would like to change your work situation?

Think: Think of one thing that you could change for the better at work.

Question: Ask people about ways they have changed their work situation.

Observe: Watch for articles about the workplace.

1: Check-in: Give an example of how you slowed down this week.

2: Reflection: Think about possible ways you could change your work.

3: Small group discussion: Talk in pairs about ways to change work.

4: Large group discussion: Go around the circle and tell your stories of the ways you would like to change work.

5: Comments: Report on ideas from personal research.

6: Action commitments: Commit to taking a small step to doing something to change your work situation.

Session Ten: Planning for the Future

Purpose: To discuss public policy issues and to decide the form the simplicity circle will take for those planning to continue.

Preparation: Review chapter 16, "What's Wrong with Wealth," and chapter 17, "Structural Changes."

Personal research: Question for the week: What societal change would bring about a reduction in people's greed?

Think: When have you been greedy in your own life? What circumstances encouraged the greed?

Question: Ask people what they would do to reduce greed if they became president.

Observe: Watch for articles on corporate behavior.

1: Check-in: Report on the action you had planned to take at work.

2: Reflection: Think about the most important thing you have learned in the nine preceding weeks.

3: Small group discussion: Talk in groups of three about what you have learned.

4: Large group discussion: Go around the circle and tell what you learned and how you would translate that into policy if you were in a leadership position.

5: Comments: The rest of the meeting should be devoted to deciding what you will do in the future.

BEYOND THE TEN WEEKS

After the first ten weeks, some people will have to stop because of other plans and some will continue. By this time, you won't need to follow such a strict format and your time will be spent in two main activities: the check-in and the comments. Discuss what form you would like to have the circle take. Do you want to invite more people to join? Do you want to meet only every two weeks, perhaps, or once a month?

The check-in activity should expand because most people are working on several different levels at once. Consider these three areas for discussion: reduce, resist, and rejoice.

Reduce: Continue to talk about how you have cut back in your consumption, reduced your physical and mental clutter, and cut back on activities that keep you from pursuing your passion.

Resist: Move into an analysis of the pressures of marketing and cultural expectations and how you can resist them. Talk more about larger cultural changes that need to take place.

Rejoice: Talk about the areas in your life that lift your spirit and make you feel joyful—and how you can increase these activities. Talk about ways you have built community, pursued your passion, learned to enjoy life more, and so on.

People can develop the circle in any way they want because by this time, they don't need more guidelines. Sometimes groups have decided to take political action together. Although it is up to the group to decide what it wants, past experience has shown that this could break up a group, because the focus is different. I recommend that study circles remain primarily as a place for people to talk. Circles should encourage people to get involved in political actions in any way they can, but perhaps not as a group. Talking is important!

AFTERWORD

JOAN'S JOURNAL ENTRY

Well, I've done it. Cut back to three-quarters time. I'm going to take every Friday off. I've given my assistants more responsibility, which they seem happy with. It feels more like we're colleagues now, rather than boss and workers.

Now the challenge is to stick to this reduced schedule. At first I thought I would get a lot of support for this move, because everyone seemed to think it was such a great idea. But now I'm beginning to pick up on a little resentment in comments like, "I wish I didn't have to work on Fridays." I was warned this might happen. People start to feel envious. Well, maybe some of them will follow my example.

Have I made a mistake? I don't know. What is a mistake, anyway? I suppose there are some people who will think I'm not serious about my career. I hope they see that what I'm serious about is my life.

But there was really nothing else I could do. Even though it turned out okay, that breast biopsy scared me, and it got me looking at things differently, asking myself what I really wanted out of life. I know several women who took early retirement when Jacqueline Onassis died of cancer.

I'm feeling a little anxious about what to do with my new free time, though. Part of me wants to take a class, but the only thing I can think of is a computer course or something for my career. God, I hope I don't get into that rut again—always focusing on my career all the time. My job had just taken over my life.

At least I'm not having that old Sunday night dread I used to get. After having Fridays off, I actually look forward to work on Monday mornings. Well, most of the time.

Maybe a bird-watching class. I'm starting to have different feelings about nature ever since I started my simplicity circle. A lot of people talk so movingly about their experiences. I've always been so focused on city things. And a bird-watching class would slow down me down. You can't rush around when you're watching birds.

I think that before I decide what to do I'll take some time to just hang out. Just sit and see what comes up. I'm glad it's summer, because I can sit in my garden and watch the birds. The other day I noticed that two little birds are building a nest in that birdhouse we hung up. They each fly out and find just the right twig to bring back. I know I can learn something about life from watching them.

But I don't want to become too self-absorbed. I've been wanting to get involved in something outside the corporate life. Something where I didn't always have to worry about my image, worry that I'd spilled something on my shirt. Maybe I'll talk to those people who started that newspaper for the homeless. I don't know, somehow the issue of homelessness strikes me as such a symbol for our times. To not have a home. What does that mean? Maybe we all feel homeless, because we don't see the earth as our home. We don't really take care of it. We're fouling our nest. (Maybe my subconscious really wants me to take that bird-watching course.)

I really like the looks on the faces of those men selling their newspaper. They're getting fifty cents for every paper they sell, but obviously they're getting a lot more than that.

I don't want to rush into anything, though. You meet those people who have just retired and they say that they're busier than they've ever been before. I don't want to keep rushing around. That was the reason I cut back. But that homeless project really attracts me. It's the idea of these people getting together and transforming things themselves. Fighting back. It would also get me around another group of people. I know I'm a yuppie, my friends are all yuppies. Having a little diversity in my life might shake me up a little.

And then there's my jewelry-making. I used to love it. Who knows, maybe I could sell some of it? If nothing else, I'll have something to give my friends—some gifts that really mean something.

But one thing I know that I'll do. Keep on going to my simplicity circle. Wednesday night is really the highlight of my week. It's been a long time since I've been so excited about something. It's great to have people who understand what I'm trying to do. So many of my friends think I'm a little crazy for trying to be frugal. They think that if I've got money, I should be spending it!

And some of the stories people tell at the simplicity circle are really funny. One woman went to a fancy black-tie wedding last week and didn't notice that she had her jacket on inside out until halfway through the evening. We all laughed so much when she told the story that we could hardly keep on with the discussion.

But I also like all the intellectual excitement. I feel like I've been kind of brain-dead for a long time. Reading memos and budget printouts doesn't really keep your mind in tip-top shape.

Joel might even start coming. He's not laughing at me as much lately when I compost our food scraps or carry my cloth bag with me when I go shopping. At first he sneered a little at the other simplicity circle members, saying they looked like granola eaters (he's really a little outdated), but when he talked to them he liked them. They're just like us; they're just looking for a way out of the rat race, a way to enjoy themselves more. Some of them have made some real changes, too. One guy, the corporate counsel, is dropping out to become a carpenter, and another woman left a high-tech company to start her own graphic design company. She says she's working even more right now, but it's so much better than playing the corporate politics.

I think having that guy at work die from a heart attack got Joel thinking. And he's kind of disgusted with the way a few of the other guys have been behaving—a couple of them broke up their long-time marriages to get involved with some young bubbleheads—talk about trophy wives. Joel says he doesn't want to end up like any of them—winding up dead or looking like a fool.

My simplicity circle is great because it's nice to have people who will listen when I feel like ranting and raving about something I read in the paper, like the new shopping mall that's going in at the north end of town. Another shopping mall! We just don't need it. How can people shop in stores that all look the same, anyway. It may cost me a little more, but I'm sticking to my neighborhood stores. Actually, I think I end up spending less, just because they don't have as much merchandise, so I don't buy as much. I used to get really sucked in by the sales! When I think of the things I bought that I didn't need because I thought I was saving money.

Now I really am saving money. I'm particularly going to save a lot because we've decided against remodeling our bathroom. I just got caught up in the excitement of all my friends remodeling theirs. And then I thought, Wait a minute. Twenty or thirty thousand dollars for a new bathroom? What's a bathroom for, anyway?

But most of all, I've been doing a lot of thinking. Trying to really figure things out. Asking myself what it is that I really need from life.

I've got a start on the frugality. Trying to live on less really does make you appreciate things more. But I want to be careful that I'm not always focusing on saving money. The point, it seems to me, is to have money move into the background of your life instead of the foreground. If you start thinking about saving money all of the time, it's almost as bad as thinking about making money all of the time.

I can see that the real answer is to focus on the things that are really fun and challenging. I'm spending a lot of time trying to figure out my passion. I really do like managing people. I am good at it. I wonder if I should think about some consulting or teaching.

What I do feel good about is that Joel and I have been following through on our plans to start having our neighbors over more, and I'm having some people from work over Friday for some wine and cheese. I think I can handle that.

But there's still a void. There's no church I've really found that I can go to. But I feel hopeful. I feel like something is stirring out there, that some big changes are coming. I get depressed sometimes thinking about the environment, but I don't know. I have a sense that things are building to a head. That people are being galvanized by the thought that some people are making a whole lot of money by ripping off nature and they're not going to take it much longer.

So it's exciting. And I'm starting to get a glimpse of a kind of peace, a hint of serenity. I think the key is to just start each day and sit. Sit and wait.

I found some passages from Thoreau the other day that I really like. I'm trying to memorize them. It's what I want to feel. I think I'm finally starting to define the good life for myself.

> I am grateful for what I am and have. My thanksgiving is perpetual. It is surprising how contented one can be with nothing definite—only a sense of existence. My breath is sweet to me. O how I laugh when I think of my vague indefinite riches. No run on my bank can drain it, for my wealth is not possession but enjoyment.
>
> If the day and the night are such that you greet them with joy, and life emits a fragrance, like flowers and sweet-scented herbs— is more elastic, starry, and immortal,—that is your success.
>
> —HENRY DAVID THOREAU

BIBLIOGRAPHY

Adbusters: Journal of the Mental Environment, published by The
    Media Foundation, Vancouver, B.C.

Bender, Sue. *Plain and Simple*. New York: Harper & Row, 1989.

Berry, Thomas. *The Dream of the Earth*. San Francisco: Sierra Club
    Books, 1988.

Borish, Steven. *The Land of the Living: The Danish Folk High
    Schools and Denmark's Non-Violent Path to Modernization*.
    Nevada City, Calif.: Blue Dolphin Publishing, 1991.

Brandt, Barbara. *Whole Life Economics*. Philadelphia: New Society
    Publishers, 1995.

Buber, Martin. *I and Thou*. New York: Scribners, 1958.

Cajete, Gregory. *Look to the Mountain*. Durango, Colo.: Kivaki
    Press, 1994.

Caldicott, Helen. *If You Love This Planet*. New York: W.W. Norton,
    1992.

Callenbach, Ernest. *Ecotopia Emerging*. Berkeley, Calif.: Banyon
    Tree Books, 1981.

Christensen, Frederik. "Nikolai Frederik Severin Grundvig: A
    Lecture Given in Tanzania in November 1983." *Option: Journal
    of the Folk Education Association of America*, fall 1987.

Cobb, Clifford; Ted Halsted; and Jonathan Rowe. "If the GDP Is
    Up, Why Is America Down?" *Atlantic Monthly*, October 1995.

Cobb, John. "Seeds of Hope." In *Voices on the Threshold of
    Tomorrow*, edited by Feuerstein & Feuerstein. Wheaton, Ill.:
    Quest Books, 1993.

Csikszentmihalyi, Mihaly. *Flow*. New York: Harper & Row, 1990.

cummings, e.e. "I thank You God for most this amazing. . . . " In *100
    Selected Poems*. New York: Grove Press, 1959.

Daly, Herman E., and John B. Cobb Jr. *For the Common Good*.
    Boston: Beacon Press, 1994.

Davis, Adelle. *Let's Have Healthy Children.* New York: Harcourt, 1951.

Davis, David. *Model for a Humanistic Education: The Danish Folk Highschool.* Columbus, Ohio: Charles E. Merrill, 1971.

de Graaf, John, and Vivia Boe, producers. *Running Out of Time* (video). Seattle: Oregon Public Broadcasting and KCTS/Seattle.

de Mille, Agnes. *Dance to the Piper.* Boston: Little, Brown, 1952.

Dominguez, Joe, and Vicki Robin. *Your Money or Your Life.* New York: Viking/Penguin, 1992.

Durning, Alan. *How Much is Enough?* New York: W.W. Norton, 1992.

Easwaran, Eknath. *The Compassionate Universe.* Petaluma, Calif.: Nilgiri Press, 1989.

Elgin, Duane. *Voluntary Simplicity.* New York: Bantam/William Morrow, 1981.

Field, Joanna (Marion Milner). *A Life of One's Own.* Boston: Tarcher/Houghton Mifflin, 1981.

Fox, Matthew. *Creation Spirituality.* San Francisco: Harper-SanFranscisco, 1991.

————. *Original Blessing.* Santa Fe, N. Mex.: Bear, 1983.

————. *A Spirituality Named Compassion.* Minneapolis: Winston Press, 1979.

Frankl, Viktor. *Man's Search for Meaning.* Boston: Beacon Press, 1963.

French, Marilyn. *Beyond Power.* New York: Summit Books, 1985.

Fromm, Erich. *The Art of Being.* New York: The Continuum Publishing Company, 1994.

————. *To Have or to Be.* New York: Harper & Row, 1976.

Frommer, Arthur. *New World of Travel, 5th Edition.* New York: Simon & Schuster Macmillan, 1996.

Gatto, John Gaylor. *Dumbing Us Down.* Philadelphia: New Society Publishers, 1992.

The Giraffe Project: A Project to Encourage People to Stick Their Necks Out for the Common Good. *Every Day Heroes.* Langley, Wash.

Glendinning, Chellis. *"My Name is Chellis & I'm in Recovery from Western Civilization."* Boston: Shambhala, 1994.

Gottlieb, Roger, ed. *This Sacred Earth.* New York: Routledge, 1996.

Gregg, Richard. *The Value of Voluntary Simplicity.* Wallingford, Pa.: Pendle Hill, 1936.

Harmon, Willis. "Changing the Self to Change the World." In *Voices on the Threshold of Tomorrow*, edited by Feuerstein & Feuerstein. Wheaton, Ill.: Quest Books, 1993.

Heilbrun, Carolyn. *Writing a Woman's Life.* New York: Norton, 1988.

Hope Magazine: Humanity Making a Difference, published by Hope Publishing, Brooklin, Maine.

Horton, Myles. *The Long Haul.* New York: Anchor/Doubleday, 1990.

Horton, Myles, and Paulo Freire. *We Make the Road by Walking.* Philadelphia: Temple, 1990.

Horton, Myles. "Speech: Denmark, 1984." *Option: Journal of the Folk Education Association of America,* spring 1988.

Jacobson, Michael F., and Laurie Ann Mazur. *Marketing Madness.* Boulder, Colo.: Westview Press, 1995.

Kahn, Michael. *The Tao of Conversation.* Oakland, Calif.: New Harbinger Publications, 1995.

Kanner, Allen, and Mary Gomes. "The All-Consuming Self." In *Ecopsychology*, edited by Theodore Roszak. San Francisco: Sierra Club Books, 1995.

Kazan, Elia. *The Arrangement.* New York: Stein and Day, 1967.

Ket, Joseph. *The Pursuit of Knowledge Under Difficulties.* Stanford, Calif.: Stanford University Press, 1994.

Kohn, Alfie. *No Contest.* Boston: Houghton Mifflin, 1986.

Lakein, Alan. *How to Get Control of Your Time and Your Life.* New York: P.H. Wyden, 1973.

Lappe, Frances Moore, and Paul Martin DuBois. *The Quickening of America.* San Francisco: Jossey-Bass, 1994.

Lehmkuhl, Dorothy, and Dolores Cotter Lamping. *Organizing for the Creative Person.* New York: Crown, 1994.

Levering, Frank, and Wanda Urbanska. *Simple Living*. New York: Viking, 1992.

McKibben, Bill. *Hope, Human and Wild*. Boston: Little, Brown, 1995.

McLaughlin, Corinne, and Gordon Davidson. *Spiritual Politics*. New York: Ballantine Books, 1994.

Mander, Jerry. *In the Absence of the Sacred*. San Francisco: Sierra Club Books, 1991.

Merchant, Carolyn. *Radical Ecology*. New York: Routledge, 1992.

Merck Family Fund. *Yearning for Balance,* July 1995.

Meyers, David. *The Pursuit of Happiness*. New York: William Morrow, 1992.

Moore, Thomas. *Care of the Soul*. New York: HarperCollins, 1992.

Ness, Arne. "The Deep Ecological Movement." In *Deep Ecology for the 21st Century,* edited by George Sessions. Boston: Shambhala, 1995.

New Road Map Foundation. *All-Consuming Passion*. Seattle: 1993.

Noddings, Nel. *Caring*. Berkeley: University of California Press, 1984.

O'Hara, Bruce. *Working Harder Isn't Working*. Vancouver, B.C.: New Star Books, 1993.

Oldenburg, Ray. *The Great Good Place*. New York: Paragon House, 1989.

O'Neil, John R. *The Paradox of Success*. New York: Tarcher/Putnam, 1993.

Ornstein, Robert, and David Sobel. *Healthy Pleasures*. Reading, Mass.: Addison-Wesley, 1989.

Orr, David. *Earth in Mind*. Washington, D.C.: Island Press, 1994.

———. *Ecological Literacy*. Albany: State University of New York Press, 1992.

Putnam, R. "Bowling Alone: America's Declining Social Capital." *Journal of Democracy,* January 1995.

Reder, Alan. *75 Best Business Practices for Socially Responsible Companies*. New York: Tarcher/Putman, 1995.

Rifkin, Jeremy. *The End of Work*. New York: Tarcher/Putnam, 1995.

Roberts, Elizabeth, and Elias Amidon. *Earth Prayers*. San Francisco: HarperSanFrancisco, 1991.

Roszak, Theodore, editor. *Ecopsychology*. San Francisco: Sierra Club Books, 1995.

————. *Voice of the Earth*. New York: Simon & Schuster, 1992.

————. *Where the Wasteland Ends*. New York: Anchor Books/ Doubleday, 1973.

Ruether, Rosemary Radford. *Gaia and God*. New York: Harper-Collins, 1992.

Ruggiero, Greg, and Stuart Sahulka, editors. *The New American Crisis*. New York: The New Press, 1995.

Saltzman, Amy. *Downshifting*. New York: HarperCollins, 1991.

Schor, Juliet. "A Sustainable Economy for the Twenty First Century." In *The New American Crisis*, edited by Greg Ruggiero and Stuart Sahulka. New York: The New Press, 1995.

————. *The Overworked American*. New York: Basic Books/ HarperCollins, 1991.

Schumacher, E. F. *Small is Beautiful*. New York: Harper & Row, 1973.

Shaffer, Carolyn R., and Kristin Anundsen. *Creating Community Anywhere*. Los Angeles: Tarcher/Perigee, 1993.

Shapiro, Andrew. *We're Number One*. New York: Vintage Books, 1992.

Shekerjian, Denise. *Uncommon Genius*. New York: Penguin, 1990.

Shi, David. *In Search of the Simple Life*. Layton, Utah: Gibbs M. Smith, 1986.

————. *The Simple Life*. New York: Oxford University Press, 1985.

Sinetar, Marsha. *Do What You Love, the Money Will Follow*. New York: Paulist Press, 1987.

Slater, Philip. *A Dream Deferred*. Boston: Beacon Press, 1991.

————. *Wealth Addiction*. New York: E.P. Dutton, 1980.

————. *The Pursuit of Loneliness*. Boston: Beacon Press, 1970.

Swan, James. "Lessons from Ring Mountain." In *Earth Keepers*, edited by Leslie Baer-Brown and Bob Rhein. San Francisco: Mercury House, 1995.

Tart, Charles. *Living the Mindful Life*. Boston: Shambhala, 1994.

Thoreau, Henry David. *Walden/Civil Disobedience*. Boston: Houghton Mifflin/Riverside Editions, 1957.

Ueland, Brenda. *Strength to Your Sword Arm*. Duluth, Minn.: Holy Cow! Press, 1993.

———. *If You Want to Write*. St. Paul, Minn.: The Schubert Club, 1938, 1983.

Walker, Alice. *In Search of Our Mothers' Gardens*. New York: Harcourt Brace Jovanovich, 1983.

Wallis, Jim. *The Soul of Politics*. New York: Orbis Books; The New Press, 1994.

Whitmeyer, Claude, editor. *In the Company of Others*. New York: Tarcher/Perigree, 1993.

Wuthnow, Robert. *Sharing the Journey*. New York: The Free Press, 1994.

Woolf, Virginia. *Three Guineas*. New York: Harcourt, Brace & World, 1938, 1968.

Yes! A Journal of Positive Futures, published by Positive Futures Network, Bainbridge Island, Wash.

ACKNOWLEDGMENTS

What a pleasant experience writing this book has been. When you get involved in the voluntary simplicity movement, you discover that the people are incredibly nice. They are warm, open, and fun to be with. So I particularly enjoy acknowledging the help I've had.

First, a salute to the pioneers of the current resurgence of this age-old movement. It was from Thoreau that I first learned of the concept of voluntary simplicity, but it was from Duane Elgin that I first heard the words. I loved getting to know Duane Elgin. So often you like an author's work and then are totally disappointed in him or her as a person. Not with Duane. Whenever I called him and said, "Do you have a minute?" he always responded with, "Of course I do." What a nice man.

Vicki Robin and Joe Dominguez are truly dedicated and committed to spreading this movement. As the press bombarded them about their bestselling book *Your Money or Your Life*, they always told them about others' work, including mine.

Thanks to Chris Spicer, the president of the Folk Education Association of America, who helped me discover this transformative method of adult learning, and to the Study Circles Resource Center in Pomfret, Connecticut, for its work to rekindle democracy through public talk.

As strange as it might seem these days, I have thank-yous for the mainstream press. Dozens and dozens of stories have been written about this movement, and almost every reporter did the story because he or she was vitally interested.

And who would have thought a major daily newspaper would publish a column called "Voluntary Simplicity." The *Seattle Times* is one of the few independent major daily newspapers around these days, and the publishers plan to keep it that way.

The Northwest is also home to two national publications that have been helpful to me: First is *Yes! A Journal of Positive Futures* (formerly

In Context, which can now be found on the World Wide Web.) *Yes!* continues to publish articles that inspire people to simplify their lives.

A journal started more recently is *Simple Living: The Journal of Voluntary Simplicity,* edited by Janet Luhrs, my partner in our local broadcasts on Seattle's National Public Radio station, KUOW.

My next thank-yous are to all the people in Seattle who came to the workshops and joined simplicity circles. My ideas come not only from theories, but from what I learned working with real people. This is truly a people's movement.

These workshops and study circles wouldn't have existed without the sponsorship of local community colleges, universities, and nonprofit groups. In particular, I want to thank the director of the University of Washington Women's Center, Sutapa Basu. She and I have been partners in social change for many years. Leslie Cossit, program director at the Phinney Neighborhood Center, has helped voluntary simplicity become visible in Seattle.

The most recent people to enter my life because of voluntary simplicity are my agent and my editor, Joel Fishman and Mauro DiPreta. If they're anything to go by, what great and interesting talkers New York men must be! They both maintain the human touch in a business I'd imagined to be cold and impersonal—and they both make me laugh. A special thank-you as well to the wonderfully helpful staff at HarperCollins.

And of course, as acknowledgments always say—I couldn't have done it without my spouse. But it's true. Being married to the high-tech reporter for the *Seattle Times* (the coauthor of *Gates*) is very lucky for someone whose very aura screws up technology. And what a copy editor he is! A page will look absolutely clean to me and he will still find lots of typos! He's also a really nice man, too. (This last sentence was periodically eliminated and reinserted throughout the various edits. Working with a spouse isn't always smooth going.)

And thank you to the most pleasant, cheerful person I know: my daughter, Rebecca, who helped me keep order in my life. (Where did she get that ability?) If I ever needed to boost my spirits, I needed only to call her.